It All Began With a Parachute Jump

a woman's life changes
through learning to fly

Published in Great Britain in 2021
by Big White Shed, Nottingham
www.bigwhiteshed.co.uk
Printed and bound
by Imprint Digital, Exeter, Devon

ISBN 978-1-9150210-0-7
Copyright © Philippa Sharp
Cover Design by Richard Heaven

A CIP catalogue record of this book is available from
The British Library.

For women everywhere, to encourage them to be bold and make a jump into new adventures and life changes.

CONTENTS

Preface 6

Chapter 1
Parachute Jump 8

Chapter 2
Trial Flight 15

Chapter 3
Flying from Manchester 28

Chapter 4
Flying from Barton 41

Chapter 5
First Solo 47

Chapter 6
Trip to Portugal 56

Chapter 7
PPL and Beyond 66

Chapter 8
G - BNTP 78

Chapter 9
IMC Rating 82

Chapter 10
Trip to Beverley 88

Chapter 11
Trip to Scotland 92

Chapter 12
Engine Problems 108

Chapter 13
Personal Problems 117

Chapter 14
Night Rating 123

Chapter 15
Single Life 142

Chapter 16
Gliding 147

Chapter 17
Manchester Bomb 154

Chapter 18
More Flying Trips 160

Chapter 19
Gordon 165

Chapter 20
Concorde 167

Chapter 21
Last Flight 172

Chapter 22
Summary and Conclusions 176

PREFACE

In July 2020 I had just finished writing my first book, "Light the Blue Touch Paper – a woman's adventures at sea". As the whole of the UK was still in Lockdown due to the Coronavirus, I needed another project. I had already planned another book about my flying adventures.

I found this book much harder to write as it is a "prequel" to my first book. It covers the period from January 1987 to September 1998 with my last flight.

During this time I was working full time, so was involved in a busy work, family and social life while also learning to fly. Although I have my Flying Logbook which gives details of my flying trips to jog my memory, I have not recounted much of my day to day life.

Compared to my sailing adventures which were mostly sunny and carefree, my flying adventures are much more about battling through prejudice and misogyny in the grey gloom of northern England, apart from the week I spent in Portugal finishing my Private Pilot's Licence (PPL) in 1992.

The world of flying clubs in England is full of men and can be extremely misogynistic. There were only a few women who flew, certainly in the 80s and 90s.

In the light of this situation, what I and other women achieved was well worth fighting for. The sheer adrenaline of taxiing down the runway and pushing the throttle in, to increase power and take off was just brilliant, looking down to see the queues of cars on the motorway as the plane soared high above them.

The positive side of writing this book is that I am renewing contact with flying friends, both men and women who still live in the north of England, whereas the sailing friends are difficult to track down – they don't stay in one place for long!

Philippa Sharp

June 2020

CHAPTER 1

PARACHUTE JUMP

Is there something you have always wanted to do, but just never got around to doing it? These days it would be called a *Bucket List*, but this book starts in 1986, before the days of bucket lists.

I had always wanted to do a parachute jump, but I was busy – running a business with my husband, two teenage daughters, elderly parents, etc. Any old excuse.

However, my eldest daughter, Sam, who was then 17, kick started the process for me. She was going to do a parachute jump but needed parent's permission, being under 18, so brought home a consent form for my signature.

Although I was happy to sign the form I was a little bit irritated. This was something I wanted to do! But it was my fault for not getting round to it. I was 39.

At one of my weekly chats with Sam during Lockdown, I asked her about her jump and the reason for it. She told me it was a challenge she set herself as she has a fear of heights. Wow. I found it pretty scary, and I wouldn't say I am frightened of heights. She also did a second jump just to prove she could do it! On the first jump she had to sit on the edge of the plane at the door and push herself off, but the second one she stood out on the strut and jumped out backwards.

Sam recalled thinking she would die after jumping out, but then when the chute opened she experienced a wonderful peaceful moment of silence. As she descended the sounds started to return, traffic, people, etc.

My own experience was very similar:

I decided to give myself a 40th birthday present of a parachute jump. There were costs involved. I applied to the Manchester Free Fall Club. I would have to attend training sessions (about 5 hours) before being signed off to do the jump.

Of course it is possible to do a "tandem" jump where you are strapped to an instructor, but that wouldn't give me any sense of achievement.

I had to go to Manchester University for the training sessions, which meant everyone else was very young! We were strung up in parachutes and learned the process of the jump. These are static line jumps. You have a line hooked to the plane which breaks when you jump out and therefore automatically opens your parachute. I'm sure you have seen old war films where men are packed into planes and move up to the open door, hook on and jump out!

However this wasn't quite the same, as we were to be in a small plane which had no seats and would only accommodate a pilot, an instructor and about five parachutists. We went through the process in training with all emergencies covered:

1. Q. What happens if the static line doesn't break?

A. An instructor climbs out onto the wing with a knife to cut you lose, otherwise the open parachute could bring the plane down!

2. Q. What happens if your chute doesn't open?

A. You have an emergency chute strapped to your front and there is a drill for this.

So **in theory** – you climb out onto the strut of the plane, you hold on looking at the instructor until he says **GO** also indicating with his arm, as it is very noisy outside a plane at 2,000 ft. You then jump and count to yourself "one thousand, two thousand, three thousand". You then look up to see if your chute has opened, although in practice you will feel it first as a jolt like putting the brakes on as it slows you down, yanking you upwards.

If the chute has not opened you go through a routine to open your emergency chute which is:

LOOK, PULL, GRAB, THROW.

1. LOOK – locate your emergency chute tied to the front of your body.

2. PULL – a line which opens the bag of the chute.

3. GRAB – take hold of the parachute inside and

4. THROW – the chute as far as you can in front of you so that it can open freely.

We were drilled many times in this procedure until it became embedded in our brains.

There is a limited amount of manoeuvrability in the basic round parachutes we used. You could pull a cord on each side which moves you to the side during descent, unlike the fancy expensive ones which are shaped more like a hang glider. These are so light that you can land standing up by pulling on a cord which slows you right down to land gently.

We also had training on how to land safely. If you land hard on the ground you can damage your spine or knees. If you land facing forwards you will roll forwards and may damage your face, or specs if like me you are a specs wearer.

So, as you are approaching the ground you will naturally be facing forwards into wind but must turn yourself so that you land backwards and ROLL over backwards and sideways throwing your legs over your shoulder.

When the instructors thought we were sufficiently trained to be ready for a jump the last session was a TEST. We went into an area one by one to be hung up in our chutes and instructors would shout different emergencies at us so that we could demonstrate the right response. Lots of **LOOK, PULL, GRAB, THROW.**

Having passed the test, we then had a day arranged for the jump. We all went by minibus to Tilstock Airfield, Whitchurch in Shropshire. Having checked that the weather was okay for a beginner's jump, we were then required to get into all the kit, boiler suit, parachute harness, emergency chute strapped to the front, and helmet before making our way into the plane which was a high wing Cessna with only one seat (for the pilot). It was probably a Cessna 172 but I didn't know much about planes at that time. There was maybe four or five of us crouched in the plane with the instructor at the front.

The jump was to be made from 2000 feet so after take-off we circled the airfield until we were at the correct height for the first jumper. After the first person had jumped we circled again, gaining height until reaching the altitude for the next person to jump. As I was the smallest person I was at the back of the plane (the roof of the plane slopes down at the back of the cockpit) so was the last to jump.

Of course, this only gave me more time for nerves to build up, watching all the others go before I crawled forward to the door, then clipped on and was instructed to climb out onto the strut of the wing and hold on. Heart pounding but not wanting to "chicken out" I waited until given the signal to jump. Then looked down, looked at instructor and hesitated before jumping (well you would, wouldn't you?). This meant that I was slightly out of the airfield perimeter and over a crop field – oops.

However, after counting one thousand, two thousand, three thousand VERY FAST I looked up and all was well. I floated gently down. Luckily as I saw the ground approaching I remembered that I was to land backwards into wind so pulled at cords to turn myself around and did land backwards rolling over gently. Hoorah.

I then had a struggle to gather up the chute and return with it to the base hut. After meeting all the others, who had all had a good experience, except one who didn't land very well and jarred her back, we went off home. I was on Cloud 9 for the rest of the day.

After this I decided I would like to do another jump. As a beginner I would have to do 10 jumps successfully from 2000 feet before progressing to higher jumps.

The Free Fall Club only operated at weekends. Some weekends when the weather was good I was busy, and when I was free the weather was dreadful. I did go down to Tilstock again thinking it might be OK for a jump. I went on my own and took the Sunday papers with me. I sat in the car reading and waiting for the wind to drop. It didn't and I drove home disappointed.

After more thought and consideration I realised that the thing I enjoyed most was being in the plane, not jumping out of it, so I decided to see if I could learn to fly.

CHAPTER 2

TRIAL FLIGHT

After my parachuting experience, I tried repeatedly to make another jump, but life, work and weather were against me. As a beginner I would have to make another jump within a period of time (I don't remember how long) or I would have to redo the training. So in the end I abandoned the idea of taking up parachuting as a hobby, and thought I would try flying instead.

One of the problems with this was that Chris, my husband had said that he wanted to learn to fly. So when I decided that I would rather fly than parachute, I waited to see if he was going to do it. It would have been far too expensive in money terms and in time, for both of us to do it at the same time. Eventually he decided he was too busy and involved with our rapidly expanding business to commit to the weekly training and study required to undertake training for a PPL (Private Pilot's Licence).

So, it was probably sometime in spring of 1989 that I phoned up to book a trial flight. I went to MSF Aviation at Manchester Airport. There were several flying clubs located on the South Side of the airport. Unfortunately, these clubs and some other related businesses had to move when the second runway was built so I was very lucky then to have the experience of flying out of a large airport in a small plane.

I had always loved flying, it was part of the holiday experience for me, but in practice I hadn't done that much.

As a child our family holidays were mostly camping as it was cheap, apart from a "house swap" when we lived in London, with another family who lived in the Lake District near Patterdale. That was a wonderful experience for me. It rained a lot, no surprise there, but we got out on the hills and enjoyed the countryside. The cottage we stayed in was in a field which was full of cows which seemed enormous to me as I was probably about 9 at the time. I was rather terrified of the cows but did not show it in order not to be teased by my older brother and sister. We made up names for them, like Woka, which was my father's pet name for chocolate, for the brown and white cow. This made it feel a little safer.

After we moved to Wilhelmshaven in Germany in 1958, my parents decided we needed some "culture" so we packed up in the summer holidays and drove round Europe seeing all the capitals. This was great but I was probably a bit too young at

11 to really appreciate all the buildings, churches and cities. I remember the three of us fighting in the back of the car and just looking forward to the next ice cream.

This holiday inevitably involved camping. So we packed the car with my father's ex- army kit, tents, tarpaulins, blankets, etc. When we arrived in what became our favourite camp site on Lake Garda in northern Italy we were in for a shock.

As my father was always keen to GET THERE we drove down from the north coast of Germany to northern Italy over the Brenner Pass with only one overnight stop in a Gasthaus. This meant we didn't have to get all our camping kit out for one night which SAVED TIME. These small Inns in Bavaria offered B&B accommodation. They had wonderful paintings on the outside walls, wooden roofs and balconies with lots of colourful geraniums. They also had lovely names, "Gasthof Zum Baren" Gasthof at the sign of the Bear, or "Gasthof Zum Lowen" Gasthof at the sign of the Lion, etc. We liked the bears best.

Once we were at the top of the Brenner Pass where there was a border post between Germany and Italy, we could get out and stretch our legs in the sunshine while our car was in a queue to get through the border checks.

My father loved Italy. He had served in the Signal

Corps with the Army during WW2 in Italy and his Italian was very good. So we felt we had arrived when we reached Italy.

Our favourite campsite was on the shores of Lake Garda at the southern end near Desenzano. There was a small pebble beach and swimming was possible in the lovely clear lake waters.

We unpacked our ex-army kit and put up our heavy canvas khaki tents. We had no sleeping bags but slept with lots of ex-army blankets, dark green coloured. When not used overnight these blankets were rolled up and put in a canvas roll bag which was our seat for meals which we ate sitting around a bread board.

As we looked around at other campers, mainly Germans, we felt very embarrassed. There were light, colourful frame tents with zipped up awnings, windows and porches. Everyone had lightweight fold up tables and chairs. Some even had tablecloths and vases of flowers on the tables which we thought was totally "over the top". The next year we had all the right kit and felt a lot better.

It was a big camp site, well laid out in square plots on rows, but the best plots were at the front overlooking the lake. We called this "Millionaire's Row". If we stayed for a week or two on this site my father would always keep an eye open for anyone leaving the front row. If there were signs of packing up, he would hover and ask if they were leaving. Then we would pick up our tents at the corners and walk them over to the new site.

Of course us kids were always a bit embarrassed by our father doing this but we really enjoyed being on the front row if we managed to get there.

***

When Chris and I went on holidays with our children we also went camping, starting in Cornwall when the girls were small then progressing to travelling on the continent.

Most of these trips were very good, but the final one in 1976 was awful. We had gone with two other families in a hired van to travel round France and northern Italy.

1976 was a famous year as there was a drought in England. This was the second hottest summer since records began. The highest temperature recorded was over 35.9 degrees C in Cheltenham on 3rd July.

The problems started because the period 1971-1975 recorded very low rainfall. This meant that by the spring of 1976 reservoirs were low and rivers were drying up.

The Drought Act was passed in August which led to widespread public rationing of water and standpipes in the streets. The effects on nature were devastating. Wildfires destroyed much of the countryside; 50,000 trees were lost in Dorset; £500 million of crops failed increasing the cost of food by 12%.

Massive swarms of seven spotted ladybirds appeared due to a lack of their aphid food supplies. The heatwave is said to have been the cause of 20% extra deaths in July and August.

Hose pipe bans happened early in the summer. We resorted to all sorts of ruses to save water. People put bricks in the loo tanks so that the volume of water in flushes was reduced, bath water was left in the bath after use so that it could be used for other purposes from watering plants (if not too soapy) or flushing the loo.

We could have done with some dry sunny weather for our camping trip on the continent.

The whole country was dry and parched with brown lawns and drooping plants when we set out. Unfortunately there was no drought in the mountainous areas of Austria and Italy. The heavens opened on a regular basis and we constantly packed up our soggy sleeping bags and moved on to try to find a dry region. The six adults were very grumpy and there was even muttering about getting a flight home, but talking to my daughters years afterwards they remembered the holiday with pleasure as they learned to play table football in the many bars and cafés we sheltered in.

***

I think the first flight I ever took was on a plane from RAF Jever our nearest RAF base to Wilhelmshaven on the German coast. I should explain that my father had got a job as headmaster of one of the Army boarding schools in Germany. In this post war period there were a lot of British Forces stationed in Germany with families, so schools were needed. In the holidays school trains would arrive taking the children back to wherever their parents were based. There was also the "UK party" which was a group of children going back to parents in the UK. One holiday I went with my brother and sister on this flight to stay with some of our cousins in England. Of course I found this experience very exciting.

My next flight was going on honeymoon to Jersey in 1966. We flew from a London airport to Guernsey as there was some problem at Jersey airport and then took a helicopter over to Jersey.

Cheap charter flights were just starting. Freddie Laker had pioneered "low cost, no frills" travel with his independent airline, Laker Airways which started in 1966, but sadly went bust in 1982 partly due to the recession but also the system whereby scheduled airlines like BEA and BOAC had a monopoly on slots at Heathrow and did their best to eliminate small independent companies.

Richard Branson started Virgin Atlantic in 1984 and Ryanair which also started at this time was followed by Easy Jet based at Luton from the early 1990s.

Our first family holiday to Tenerife by charter flight was in January 1978. We took a cheap deal which offered the flight and a hotel for two adults and two children. The deal did not specify the hotel but guaranteed a minimum standard of accommodation including meals and a swimming pool. However a couple of weeks before we departed we were advised that the minimum accommodation in the rooms would be one double bed and one single bed which the children were expected to share. The family who were coming with us pulled out at this stage.

We decided to risk it and took with us a sleeping pad and sleeping bag so if we got the minimum, one child could sleep on the floor. When we arrived at the hotel in Bajamar our bags were last off the coach. We feared the worst. All the large rooms would be gone by the time we got to the reception.

However although the rooms had indeed been allocated, we were given an apartment on the hotel site with 2 bedrooms, a living room, kitchen, bathroom and terrace. Wonderful. We did keep quiet about this luck, as we discovered later in the week that there were other families who had been allocated the minimum sleeping arrangements.

The airport we flew into was Los Rodeos in the north of Tenerife. At the time it was the only airport in Tenerife, but as it was 600m above sea level and situated in the damp cloudy conditions of the mountains it often suffered from poor visibility. A new airport was being built on the south coast.

We travelled around the island and went up the mountain of Teide where the top was above the clouds. We also went to the south coast which was still a desert. We saw the building work on the new airport and heard about the plans to transform this desert into a holiday resort with sandy beaches and hotels. This seemed rather a tall order at the time but 40 years later it is a very popular holiday destination partly due to the lack of rainfall and sunny conditions in the south of the island.

***

Los Rodeos was the scene of an aircraft disaster known as the "Crash of the Century" on 27th March 1977. A bomb at Gran Canaria had closed the airport there. In bound flights were diverted to Los Rodeos including two Boeing 747 aircraft which were the first of a new type of wide-bodied jets known as "jumbo jets" due to their size. These two planes were a KLM flight and a Pan Am flight.

The airport was not used to handling such large jets and had a full quota of aircraft waiting to go to Gran Canaria. As the airport was packed with planes, exits from the runways were blocked.

The KLM flight was running out of time for Pilot hours and anxious to get going. They requested re-fuelling in order to speed up their turnaround in Gran Canaria. This full fuel load meant the aircraft was heavier and needed a longer take off run.

It then started to rain and a dense fog closed in making the aircraft invisible to the tower. Because of runway congestion departing planes needed to taxi down the runway then make a 180 degree turn at the end for take- off.

The Pan Am plane missed their turn off due to poor visibility, although the next turn off was not far, it meant being on the runway for a few extra seconds. They were asked to report when they had cleared the runway.

The KLM crew were tired, annoyed and anxious. The captain failed to register that the Pan Am plane had not yet cleared the runway. They had received ATC route clearance but not take off clearance. The captain believed he had clearance to take off and started to accelerate down the runway. Both crew realised too late that they were heading towards each other and tried to avoid contact with Pan Am turning left to try to get off the runway and KLM trying to take off over them.

The result was the death of 583 passengers and crew. Amazingly 61 people including all the air crew on the Pan Am flight survived.

After this accident there was a review of air traffic control procedures and changes were made to ensure that the pilots read back the clearance to the tower to make sure there were no misunderstandings.

***

The first long haul flight I went on was in 1986. Our mobile communications business was doing well so Chris and I were invited to a meeting of BT's distributors to have a celebratory dinner and see which company had won the sales awards. The top prize was a trip to Hong Kong and Macau to see the Formula 3 motor racing. The second prize was a weekend in Paris.

We were very busy at the time with running the business and family. I was not really keen to go away for a long trip so would have been quite happy to go to Paris or just stay at home. However we won the top prize - we had had a particularly good last quarter of sales. I had never been out of Europe at that time. I wondered how I would cope with being on a flight for 24 hours as I am rather claustrophobic. We had about a week to organise things in the business and at home in order to go. Luckily my parents were living in Manchester during this period so were able to look after Sam and Melanie.

I went to the doctor's surgery to check which vaccinations we needed. They were a little grumpy with me although that was normal for the Barlow Medical Centre, I really think they felt patients were just an inconvenience in their lives. They asked me what date we were flying and then tut tutted a lot about having left it late to come to them. However when I explained that we had won the trip as a prize they did soften a little.

It was a wonderful trip. A group of around 20 of us stayed in one of the best hotels in Hong Kong and got first class service with trips around Hong Kong and on mainland China. Excellent dinners and lots of champagne at the motor racing day in Macau.

After that trip I made many more long haul trips to the Far East and to Australia and New Zealand. The flight was always part of the holiday for me.

MSF AVIATION

The planes used at MSF were Piper Tomahawk PA38 two seater low wing aircraft. I don't really remember very much about the trial flight. It was very exciting and I was all set just to sit back and relax, but the instructor with me got me handling the controls and putting me through various exercises like flying "straight and level". He seemed a bit impatient with me when I didn't immediately understand where the controls were and what I was supposed to do.

It was only a short flight, maybe half an hour.

When I arrived back I was taken into a room in the office of the MSF portakabin and lectured for what seemed like ages about the lessons needed to gain my PPL. I hadn't really thought that far ahead, but was impressed to think that he thought me capable of doing this.

I guess it was just a good sales job really, but I think I had signed up before I left the club that day. I had booked a date for my first flying lesson.

CHAPTER 3

FLYING FROM MANCHESTER

A BRIEF HISTORY OF MANCHESTER AIRPORT.

Manchester Council was keen to have a Municipal Airport so in 1935 building work started at Ringway, near Wythenshawe. This was an old RAF base.

On 25th June 1938 Ringway Airport was officially opened and scheduled flights started.

But from 1939 – 45 there were no scheduled flights due to the Second World War. The airport became a manufacturing centre with Fairey Aviation and Avro. There were 3 new runways and 10 new hangars. It was also a Training Centre for 60,000 parachutists.

In 1946 after the war, passenger services resumed and by 1947 more than 34,000 passengers per year were using the airport.

In 1951 the main runway was extended to 1798 meters and in 1962 a new terminal was built. It was the first in Europe to have a "pier" system.

By 1980 half a million passengers a month were using the airport.

The runway extended to 3048 metres in 1981

leading to the start of long haul flights.

A second runway opened in February 2001. Manchester is still the only UK airport apart from Heathrow to have two runways. Gatwick operates as a single-runway airport, with its northern runway only used if its main one is out of action for any reason.

After buying East Midlands Airport and Stansted (in 2013) MAG (Manchester Airports Group) was now the UK's largest airport operator with three Terminals and a retired Concorde G-BOAC in its own hangar at the Visitor Centre on the south side of the airport.

Although I am writing this in 2020 while in Lockdown due to the Coronavirus Pandemic, I am fortunate to have my Pilot's Flying Log as a memory aid, so I can say that I had my first training flight on 9.9.89. Details recorded in the log are date, time, aircraft type/registration, captain/ holder's operating capacity/from – to/ time of departure and arrival/ flight time (which is different) and remarks.

I will explain this as much as I can in case you are interested enough to continue with this journal and will therefore understand some of the details referred to on future flights:

9.9.89 PA38 G-BNES SIXSMITH Pu/t Manchester/ Manchester 14.30 16.25 Dual P2 .55 Ex 1-3

This tells you is that the instructor was in charge, his surname was Sixsmith. This is my logbook, so my status is Pu/t (pilot under training). We flew from Manchester and returned to Manchester. We called up for departure at 14.30 and we landed/ closed down at 16.25. I logged 55 minutes as a pilot under training on a single engine plane and we completed exercises 1, 2 and 3.

Ok this may sound like "it's all Greek to me!" So some explanation:

The registration of the plane was Golf – Bravo November Echo Sierra. The first letter, G means that the plane is British registered.

Brief details of the PPL Syllabus Exercises

Exercise 1 – Familiarisation with the aeroplane, emergency drills

Exercise 2 – Preparation for and action after flight

Exercise 3 – Air experience- flight exercise

So in reality, having signed out in the clubhouse showing a record of plane/registration/persons on board/destination you go out onto the apron to find your plane. There is then an exhaustive series of checks on the internal and external aspects of the plane. When you start you will work from a check list, but as you get familiar with this procedure it will become second nature and embedded in your brain, particularly if you fly the same type of plane or have your own plane.

I can recommend this if you have difficulty sleeping as I find learning and brain work is much more tiring than physical exercise.

After the checks I got into the plane with the instructor. The plane is dual control but as the student pilot I sat in the left-hand seat. It is always clear who has control, so the instructor will tell the student "you have control" when necessary.

The first thing we do is call up ground control on the VHF. At Manchester there are different frequencies for ground, departure, take- off and landing. At smaller airfields there will be one frequency for everything. We state where we are and request taxi to the hold for runway 24 for flight to ....

e.g. Ground this is GBNES (Golf Bravo November Echo Sierra) on the Southside requesting taxi to the hold for runway 24.

When I flew from Manchester the runways were 24/06 – this has changed now due to changes in magnetic fields. The wind in the UK is predominately from the SW so 24 is used much more than 06.

At this point the student starts paying (which is why flying from Manchester Airport is so expensive!). We will then probably be cleared to taxi to a hold point on the airfield to await further instructions.

Since the Tenerife two jumbo jets collision all messages must be repeated back to make sure you have heard the instructions correctly. Before that crash pilots could confirm with "wilco" which means received and understood, but ground control did not know what the pilot had heard and understood. The expression "wilco" was first used by the Army in 1938 meaning "will comply".

"GBNES cleared to taxi to the hold for runway 24" QNH … QFE…". The plane could now begin to taxi to the hold. QNH and QFE are the current pressure settings to put in your altimeter so that all planes are flying at the right height with the same readings.

QNH is sea level pressure, QFE is air pressure at current ground level, so if you put QFE into your altimeter you should have a reading of zero when waiting to taxi. These numbers are important as when landing and taking off you should have your altimeter set for QFE but once away from the airfield you will be instructed to change to QNH in order to accurately see heights of hills shown on the chart. When coming back into land you must set QFE again so that you land on the runway! For example Manchester airport is 250 feet above sea level whereas Barton airfield is only 86 feet above sea level.

I would always fly with a clip board on my lap and write down instructions so I could read them back correctly.

At the hold small planes would have to wait on the south side of the runway while large commercial jets would be given priority to take off on the north side. A large plane will generate a lot of air turbulence behind it when building up to take off speed down the runway, so the air traffic controller will space planes out so allowing the air turbulence to dissipate.

A small plane could be flipped over if following closely behind a jumbo jet on a day with little wind.

So we waited at the hold. This can be very exciting for aeroplane enthusiasts like me, watching planes taking off and landing, especially if you get something really unusual like Concorde, but ultimately it becomes frustrating if you have limited time for your lesson and you are paying for the total time.

I always had a passion for watching planes. When my daughters were young we often went to Bruntwood Park in Cheadle. There was an adventure playground in the park which the girls and their friends enjoyed and a café where we could linger over cups of tea, but the thing I enjoyed most was the extreme proximity to Manchester airport. Planes would come over on final approach so I could happily sit and watch them coming low over our heads while the children played.

When cleared for take- off, you would be instructed to change frequency from "ground" to "departure" for take- off and departure from runway 24. After the frequency change you call up again with call sign and position requesting take off. You will then need to have your pen (or memory) ready as you will be given your take-off clearance which you will be required to read back. E.g. "G-ES is cleared to take off, 24 departing the zone to the south via the Wilmslow Crewe railway line not above .... Feet on the QNH ..... squawk .....".

The squawk is a four-digit code which you set on your transponder when requested to do so. The controller can then see you on his/her radar screen, as long as you are in the Manchester zone.

I remember being told the importance of turning the transponder off while setting the code, then turning it on again. This is important because there are standard transponder codes meaning different things, e.g. 7500 means "I have been hijacked" so if you flicked through these numbers while changing the transponder to the code requested you could inadvertently cause an emergency response.

Most training flights from Manchester would go south to the Cheshire and Shropshire area out of the Manchester zone so that you can carry out the next exercises:

Further PPL exercises:

Exercise 4 – Effects of Controls (in flight)

Exercise 5 – Taxiing

These were completed on my second lesson from Manchester, followed by further exercises when we flew away from the airfield.

Exercise 6 - Straight and level

Exercise 7 - Climbing

Exercise 8 - Descending

Exercise 9 - Turning

After the student is proficient at these they progress to:

Exercise 10A - Slow flight

Exercise 10B - Stalling

Exercise 11. Spin avoidance

I am only giving brief details of the exercises on the PPL course. There is a lot more detail online if you are interested. There is a NOTE at this point that *at least two hours of stall awareness and spin avoidance flight training shall be completed during the course.*

I note that the times I worked on these are duly noted in red by my instructors in my logbook.

Between September 1989 and August 1990 I flew out of Manchester airport 24 times. I had a variety of instructors at this time, a total of 8 different ones, most of them I do not remember, but the best ones were Ed Pape who was the boss of MSF and Gary (keep the nose pointing down) Robinson who was my instructor for 11 flights during July and August 1990.

This maybe a little misleading, as there are 33 flights logged in my logbook for this period, but if I landed at other airfields this is logged as two separate flights. During my flying training from Manchester I only landed at one other airfield, which was Sleap in Shropshire.

CIRCUITS AT SLEAP

The next stage of training which included take off, landing and circuits could not be completed at Manchester airport as the airport was far too busy with commercial flights to allow small single engine planes to take off and land, so we would fly to Sleap airfield in Shropshire to complete these.

Exercise 12 – Take off and climb to downwind position

Exercise 13 – Circuit, approach and landing

Exercise 12/13E - Emergencies

The problem was that by the time you had managed to take off from Manchester and get to Sleap there was very little time to do many circuits and return to Manchester during your lesson.

At first we would do "touch and go" landings where you fly the plane down on to the runway so that the wheels touch, then accelerate along the runway and take off again. In this way you could get lots of practice at landing and taking off without having to get off the runway and queue up to get on and take off again.

These exercises included many emergency procedures because it was all leading up the next big milestone which is the **FIRST SOLO. EX. 14.**

I loved flying from Manchester and was very grateful for the experience, which is not available now to PPL students due to the addition of the second runway and lack of flying clubs there. I was always confident in speaking to the air traffic controllers as I had started my flying training using the procedures at a major commercial airport.

Moments I remember - coming in on finals and being asked if I could expedite as there was a 747 behind me. We looked round anxiously to see a large jumbo jet breathing down our tail. It was difficult to expedite as we had the throttle fully open and couldn't go any faster!

Coming back in "down wind" and seeing Concorde just landing on the runway.

Flying frequently with one instructor who always said "keep the nose pointing down" continually as I was coming in to land. These things stick in your brain. We used to call him Gary "keep the nose pointing down" Robinson. It is important to keep the nose down so that you maximise your speed and don't stall near the ground where a recovery may not be possible.

GROUND SCHOOL

Students also had to take exams in Aviation Law, Meteorology, Aircraft General, Navigation, Airplane Technical, Human Performance and RT (radio telephony). There were some classes at MSF in the evenings. This gave me a chance to meet other students. Two in particular – Ruth and Gordon, became friends.

The people learning to fly came from a variety of

backgrounds, Ruth was a nurse and Gordon was an engineer.

At first my plan was to blitz through the exams and get them done, but then I found out that when you took your final flight test all your exams had to be "current" i.e. taken within the last 12 months. So in my situation it was better to leave them until I had progressed further with the flight training, otherwise I would end up having to take exams again.

The exams were fairly easy. Mostly multiple-choice questions. The pass mark was 70%. I remember once getting 80% and my instructor said, "well, that was 10% wasted effort". There were also lots of ways of remembering the lists of checks involved in flying. When going into an exam on one occasion my instructor said "don't forget RTFQ". I asked him what that stood for as I hadn't heard it before.

READ THE F...... QUESTION.

A very useful thing to remember in all exams as I am a person who rushes into things enthusiastically and should remember to spend time reading the question before putting pen to paper.

In the evenings it was quiet at Manchester Airport. We would look at the large planes on the apron on the North Side of the airfield and wonder if we could go across there and fly one? We thought the controls would be similar to our small prop planes, but how would we start them?

The best lessons were RT with one of the air traffic controllers at the airport. It was very interesting. Our instructor was a pilot as well and would tell us about his experiences in flying a light aircraft from Manchester Airport. One thing I remember was that he told us to always listen to your gut feel when flying. He was once waiting at the end of the runway to be cleared for take-off and felt unsettled. He decided not to fly and called up the tower to ask for clearance to return to the South Side. His passengers were not happy, but it is always better to be on the ground wishing you were in the air than to be in the air wishing you were on the ground! Luckily I have never had to do that.

At this time I was working full time as a director and company owner in a business with my husband. We also had two teenage daughters. Although I managed to get a flying lesson in most weeks, I had not progressed to the first solo and beyond, so after about 12 months I decided to move to Barton Airfield to continue flying training.

CHAPTER 4

FLYING FROM BARTON

Barton Aerodrome is officially called City Airport Manchester on my A-Z. It is on Liverpool Road, the A57 at Barton, Eccles very near the M60 and Manchester Ship Canal. If you are driving north on the M60 turn to look left (passengers only!) when going over the bridge which spans the Ship Canal and you will see it on the left hand side.

A BRIEF HISTORY OF BARTON AERODROME.

Barton was the first municipal airfield in the UK to be licenced by the Air Ministry. The control tower and original hangar are now Grade II listed and remain in operation.

The airport opened on 29.1.30.

By May 1930 regular scheduled flights were operated by Imperial Airways three times a week to London's Croydon Airport via Castle Bromwich Aerodrome, Birmingham.

In 1934 KLM flew in from Holland to assess suitability for regular flights. The pilot stated the airfield was too small and from a meteorological standpoint (fog) this is the worst airfield in Europe.

The airfield is on the edge of Chat Moss and having mainly grass runways suffers from occasional periods of water logging, although works to improve drainage have had some success in recent years.

KLM then visited Ringway airport and of course the rest is history. Being situated 250 feet above sea level made a big difference.

During 1934/5 services were established to Belfast and Glasgow from Croydon via Barton. Also from Barton to Liverpool, Blackpool and the Isle of Man.

However in June 1938 scheduled services moved to Ringway to go upwards and out of the grass, mud and fog but Barton remained a centre for flying training and a helicopter base.

I have explained the reasons for leaving Manchester Ringway in chapter 3 so here is a brief summary of the advantages and disadvantages of flying from Barton.

It was considerably cheaper to fly per hour. As a member of the club all landing fees were free. It is a small airfield so very quick to get to your plane and fly (after ground checks of course). There is only one frequency for air traffic so not much waiting for clearance to taxi and take off.

Barton is in the Manchester area flying zone controlled by Manchester Airport so you needed to stay below 2000 feet before getting out of their zone but you could fly straight out to the North West to start training exercises. Circuit height when I was flying out of Barton was at 800ft, but I now understand that it is 1000 feet.

There was also a *Low Level Route* from Barton out to Warrington and then south avoiding the Manchester Zone. You were supposed to call up Manchester to give your details and may be given a squawk to set on the transponder.

There is a club house and bar so it is a very sociable area, also an outside seating area where on fine days you could sit outside with a beer and watch planes landing and taking off. Some pilots – mostly the blokes, although let's be honest there weren't many women flying in those days – would criticise landings. There was one pilot who was famous for his "bounced" landings. I remember someone once shouting "charge him for every landing" as he kangarooed down the runway. However there are many sayings in flying circles and one is "every landing you walk away from is a good landing".

There are two main disadvantages to flying from Barton:

1. Length of runway - 641 metres.

2. Condition of airfield.

The runway at Barton is very short compared to Manchester Airport. At Manchester you cannot see the end of the runway when you are at the beginning, due to a slight rise in the middle, however you could probably take off and land several times in a light aircraft before you reached the end.

At Barton you need to get the plane down at the beginning of the runway in order to have time to stop before you reach the hedge at the end. This rather focusses the mind to make sure you have the space to slow down. It does of course make you a better pilot.

The main runway was 27/09. It was wide so you could be instructed to use the left or right side for take-off and landing. The reason for this brings me on to the condition of the airfield. Barton is low lying and next to an area called Barton Moss. The runways are just grass strips so very weather dependent, hence the reason for using either left or right side. At wet times in the winter flying may be suspended if it was too wet and muddy, or just "touch and go" procedures banned to stop further damage.

Another big change for me was that the training planes at Barton were Cessna 150 and 152s. These are high wing aircraft which are very "forgiving". They love flying and just want to float and float rather than land. But they are very good for short runways as they take off and land at a lower speed than the Piper PA 38 I had been flying at Manchester. The wing flaps are large, it used to be known as "opening the barn doors" when you were using full flap.

My first lesson from Barton on 4.9.90 is listed as "type familiarization". So lots more to learn when doing outside and inside checks on a new aircraft type plus the different controls when inside. I grew to love the Cessnas. One big advantage of the high wing was that you could look out of the window downwards which was particularly helpful especially in a turn. However you did need to be quite agile to climb up to the wings when checking the fuel contents as the tank openings are on the tops.

I also needed knowledge of the local area, which unfortunately was mostly flat and grey. Although I had lots of different flying instructors I settled in with Mon Makan. It works well when you get on with your instructor. Mon was a small guy and with me being a small woman we did have some problems when I had to do stall practice.

In order to stall the plane you must put on the carb heat, close the throttle thus stopping the engine, then pull back on the control column which lifts the nose until the air speed drops and the stall warner sounds. A very alarming noise. Then you put the nose down to avert the stall and recover air speed. So when doing the stalling exercises I would pull the control column as hard as I could desperately trying to get the Cessna to stall, but it didn't want to, so Mon would have to pull as well on his control column in order to get the stall warning going.

From September 90 until February 91, I worked hard on circuits at Barton, everything from weather to runway direction had to be right before the instructor could get out and leave the student to do their first solo circuit.

CHAPTER 5

FIRST SOLO

I tried to get a flying lesson every week. As I was an owner and director of a business with my husband this made managing my time easier. Regular lessons help to keep things fresh, however the main problem in Manchester was usually the weather.

As I drove from my office in Stretford down to Barton I would anxiously survey the clouds. While driving over the M60 Ship Canal Bridge there is an excellent view of the surrounding area, so I could get an idea of the lesson content. It needed to be clear weather with good visibility for me to be allowed to do my first solo.

On 5th February 1991 the weather looked good, but as I got into the car park at Barton I quickly realised there was a problem. Wind direction. The planes were taking off on runway 09, which meant that after take-off you would be heading towards the motorway bridge and the city centre. This was not ideal for a first solo as any engine problem would mean coming down in a built-up area.

As I met Mon, I stated ruefully, "right weather, wrong runway".

But luckily Mon knew me well. I am not a typical

flying student who are mostly young men with more confidence than ability. I was then in my 40s and had lots of flying hours in my logbook. Mon said he would go and talk to the Chief Flying Instructor.

He came back with a smile on his face. I had been given permission to do my first solo on 09.

Even writing this now in 2020 I can sense the nervousness I was feeling, but Mon had confidence in me so I knew I would be fine. We signed out, checked the plane – <u>very carefully</u> and took off. The instructor will accompany the student first in a circuit to make sure everything is OK. The student will then park up to let the instructor out and call up the tower for clearance to taxi for take-off.

Mon went up into the control tower so that he could see my plane and presumably stand by to contact me if I had a problem, but everything went fine, although I actually did two circuits.

As I took off on the first circuit I was well aware that the only person who was going to get this plane down was me! But everything I had been trained to do was in my head. So take off, raise flaps, turn into cross wind, then turn down wind, do checks, radio calls, cross wind again and turn onto finals. Line up with runway, lower flaps as required, reduce speed gradually on finals.

As I was coming in to land on finals, I glanced

down and thought I was too far from the ground. When the plane is near enough to the ground, you pull back the throttle, thus reducing the speed and lifting the nose in a "flare" which causes the main wheels to touch down gently first. When they are on the ground you can then lower the nose to bring the small nose wheel onto the ground.

A split second decision meant I called the tower "Golf Uniform Bravo, going round" then pushed the throttle in to apply power and climb away from the runway. Mon told me afterwards he thought I was fine to land the first time, but I am a cautious person so went round the circuit and did it again!

SUCCESS. I had my first solo in my logbook. The only problem is you only get logged with 15 minutes for a first solo and there is no way I did two circuits in that time, however it was a good landing. I was well aware of everyone watching me and wanted to prove myself as a pilot.

There was a lot of male chauvinism at Barton so women pilots needed to be better than men, which we often were. We were called "split arsed pilots" which was typical of the rude remarks made to women.

***

I continued my flying training for another year at Barton, mostly flying with Mon. I flew solo on another 3 occasions in the circuit making sure I was getting confident in handling the plane when I was on my own.

The next exercises were consolidating the circuit practice and handling emergencies.

Exercise 15 – Advanced turning which included steep turns, stalling and recovery in the turns, also recovery from unusual attitudes including spiral dives

Exercise 16 – Forced landing without power

Exercise 17 – Precautionary landing

I was now ready to progress to making a flight to another airfield.

Exercise 18A - Navigation Flight Planning

This covered the procedures before making a flight – weather forecast, map selection, choice of route, controlled airspace, radio frequencies to be used were noted down, prohibited areas, etc.

My first landing away from Barton was in August 1991 when I planned and flew to Halfpenny Green, together with my instructor, Mon Makan.

Halfpenny Green aerodrome was originally built for the RAF and opened in 1941. It is now a thriving base for general aviation operators including flying schools for fixed wing and helicopters. The aerodrome is 7 miles SW of Wolverhampton and 20 miles from Birmingham.

There are 3 runways with both hard surfaces and grass.

Circuit height is 1000 feet LH (left hand) for fixed wing and 800 feet RH (right hand) for rotary.

Most small airfields have 1000 feet circuit height, Barton is an exception to this as the circuit height is 800 feet. You can do an overhead join at 1500ft but the Manchester Control Zone above Barton is from 2000 – 3500 feet so if you are flying away from Barton you must not climb above 2000 ft.

In order to fly south from Barton you could navigate west to Warrington turning over the centre at the church spire then heading south along the Low Level Route. This is a corridor for light aircraft on SVFR (Special Visual Flight Rules) flights where planes are permitted to fly in a Control Zone without having to fly IFR (Instrument Flight Rules). It has a maximum altitude of 1250 ft on the Manchester QNH and is fairly narrow, so pilots needed to be vigilant for other aircraft flying north.

Exercise 19 – Basic instrument flight

During this period of training I started on some basic instrument flying. For this exercise the student wears a pair of 'foggles'. Only the instruments on the dash-board were visible, no outside view could be seen. It taught the student to feel what was happening to the aircraft and rely on what the instruments are telling you. It required great concentration and was very tiring.

N.B. Foggles are a type of spectacles with the lenses covered up so that you cannot see out. There are also a different type which are worn for instrument flying. These have 'blinkers' at the sides, similar to those worn by horses. This means that the student can only see the instrument panel and not the view outside the plane.

Although as a student you are only permitted to fly in VFR (Visual Flight Rules) it is useful to have some training on instruments as it helps to improve your flying ability and also makes it easier to manage if you do get into cloud unexpectedly.

To operate in Visual Flight Rules you must be outside controlled airspace, under 10,000 ft, in good visibility and in sight of the surface. You should then be able to navigate by using ground features and landmarks and use scanning to avoid collisions.

***

Most flying instructors had other jobs or will be building their hours to become a commercial pilot. Mon Makan was building hours so there came a time when he was not available as an instructor.

I then flew with Phil Dean. I did not enjoy flying with this instructor. He treated me like a young male trainee with more confidence than ability. He did not allow me to handle the plane myself and would often just take over the controls and pull sharply up, down or side to side to demonstrate a point. This could be quite alarming.

I was now coming up to doing my first solo navigation flight where I would have to fly away from Barton to a navigation point and return.

I hadn't flown for a couple of weeks probably due to poor visibility for VFR flight, so Phil decided to give me a check out first before my solo navigation. He did the usual taking control when I was coming in to land even though I was perfectly capable of landing the plane myself and he got me thoroughly flustered. So when getting out of the plane, he asked me how I felt to fly the plane away from the airfield. I said I felt anxious. "Good" he said "that should sharpen your mind" and walked back to the club house.

I believe that a good instructor should aim to build a student's confidence and therefore increase their skills and abilities, not deliberately making them nervous, but not all instructors can do this.

The navigation point which I had to find was called Gathurst, slightly to the north west of Wigan. It is a meeting of the M6, a railway and a river. I knew approximately where it was but did not definitely see it. Of course I reported-in my success and had been in the air for the required length of time before landing back safely to Barton.

Most other students I talked to had had the same trouble, however I was driving down the M6 many years later and suddenly saw it. Eureka. It did exist but was much easier to see from the motorway than from 2000 feet up in a light aircraft.

Around this time I went on a business course which was about time management and planning. It was a full day's course and very interesting. At the concluding session we had to make future plans.

What did we want to achieve over the next 5 years?

What did we want to achieve over the next year?

What was the one thing which was our priority to get done in the next month?

All I could think about on this course was not a business aim, but to get my PPL.

In order to get a Private Pilot's Licence you need

to complete all the exercises satisfactorily, have a minimum of 45 hours flying time including 10 hours solo and have passed all the ground school exams within the 12 month period before your final Flight Test.

At this point in September 1991 I had been flying for 2 years; I had 67 hours 40 minutes flying P2 (pilot under training) and 2 hours 50 minutes as P1 (in command). I had passed all my ground school exams but would have to take Aviation Law again, as it was "out of time".

The frustrations of cost and time constraints at Manchester Airport had now become the weather frustrations of not being able to do enough solo flight from Barton.

Time was ticking away. My student friends were starting to qualify and I needed to make a change. Winter would arrive soon with the dark days and bad weather causing visibility problems.

I got through to January 1992 with an increase in my log of only four hours flying time, one hour of these was as P1.

I realised that this was time for a change.

CHAPTER 6

TRIP TO PORTUGAL

When the second runway was built at Manchester Airport, the flying clubs and other businesses on the south side of the runway had to move. The club I had started flying with, MSF Aviation moved part of their operation to Portugal and became MSF Aviation Algarve.

The business was still owned and run by Ed Pape who was a great instructor. I phoned him up for a discussion of my current situation.

I needed to complete three final tests to obtain my PPL.

1. Qualifying Cross Country

2. Navigation Flight Test

3. General Flight Test

I wanted to know if Ed thought it would be possible for me to complete these within a week's flying from his base in Faro Airport.

He said it would be possible, so I booked a week in Faro at the end of March 1992. I told Ed that I wouldn't go home without the PPL qualification. If I didn't pass I would extend my stay until I had passed!

Luckily Chris did not suggest he came with me. It was a good time of year to get out of England, but I felt I needed to go on my own in order to concentrate on the task in hand with no distractions. I had a lot of work to do in terms of flying hours, tests and studying. If Chris had come we would have turned the week into a holiday going out in the evenings for meals and wine. Lovely yes, but I only gave myself a week to finish the PPL and would have been annoyed if I had failed or not completed the course in that time.

I arrived in Faro on 22.3.92. Ed met me and took me to my accommodation in a small holiday complex near the airport. Although the weather was clear and sunny it had not really warmed up for the summer yet, so there were not many tourists around. A perfect time to get lots of flying from Faro Airport.

We arranged a time when Ed would collect me in the morning and I went to a local supermarket to get some essentials for my week's stay. There was an outdoor swimming pool at the complex so I decided I would swim in the morning before breakfast in order to wake up and be alert for a busy day.

I certainly did wake up! The swimming pool was freezing. Ed and others at the club thought I was mad to swim at this time of year, but having started this daily routine I continued it for the whole week.

It was a busy and hardworking week. MSF Aviation had two training planes Piper Tomahawk PA 38, the type I had started flying in Manchester, G-BGSI and G-BGKY. MSF Aviation in Manchester had been a larger operation with at least six PA 38s. I have checked in my logbook and one of the planes in Faro, G-BGKY I had flown in Manchester.

Planes are always known by their last two letters, so G-BGKY was called Golf Kilo Yankee. This is because when you first call up the tower for a flight clearance you use the full call sign, but after this you can revert to G-KY unless there happens to be another plane with the same last two letters. This would be very rare and I have not known it happen when I was flying.

At MSF Aviation in Manchester, one of the planes was G-BGRR (Golf Bravo Golf Romeo Romeo). You would get some suppressed giggles when flying this plane as it was known as Golf Romeo Romeo, so lots of "wherefore art thou?" jokes.

My first few days were spent on revision, getting used to flying Tomahawks after the Cessnas at Barton and also getting used to the local area. The first day we flew to Portimao a small airfield along the coast to the west of Faro.

The weather was wonderful, clear and sunny, such a change from Manchester and the Lancashire area. I also did more circuits and stall spin awareness. It is important NOT to get into a stall or spin but to be aware of the signs when this may happen and how to get out of it.

On the second day I flew for 1.35 hours including 45 minutes of stall spin awareness (Ex 10 + 11) which this time also had compass turns and "unusual attitudes".

For compass turns, the DI (direction indicator) would be covered up and the student has to turn onto a heading using only the compass, which floats around unlike the DI which is steady. It is necessary to stop the turn before you reach the compass heading otherwise you will go past it.

Unusual attitudes is a procedure where the student's eyes are covered while the instructor changes the instruments also making the student disorientated by the plane turning, descending and climbing. When the 'foggles' (these ones covering the eyes completely) are removed, the student must quickly realise what is happening and adjust the power and attitude of the plane to correct.

The plane could be descending fast in a turn (which could result in a spin) or climbing slowly with low power (which could result in a stall). All very exciting and requiring fast reactions.

By day four I did a solo flight navigating from Faro to Portimao and back in the morning and then did my Navigation Flight Test in the afternoon.

NAVIGATION FLIGHT TEST

26th March 1992

The student is asked to plan a flight from the home airport to Point A then on to Point B and back to the starting point in a triangular pattern. This involves sitting in the classroom and planning all aspects of the flight in case questions are asked. The completed flight plan will have headings, distances, timings and weather/wind directions.

However in practice you will not reach Point B because after you have found Point A the instructor will ask the student to put on the foggles while they disorientate you and change the instrument settings. When you take off the foggles you will be asked to indicate to the instructor where you are on the map – then asked to navigate to Point X giving an estimated time of arrival.

I think this was the hardest thing I ever had to do. I had been given a tip – when the foggles go on you put your finger on the map at the point where you are and check the time, so that you know within a radius of that point where you can be.

Before saying where you are you must check the instruments. Often the DI (direction indicator) will need re-aligning with the compass or the AI (attitude indicator) will have been altered. Also check the power to make sure you are in level flight, not climbing or descending.

So having checked everything and looking out of the window for visual orientation, I said to Ed Pape where I thought I was. However Ed was in "stern CAA examiner" mode, not "helpful instructor" mode so he neither confirmed nor denied this information, which was very unsettling. Was I right or not?

So the only thing I could do was to assume I was right and proceed to get out my ruler on the map and measure the distance to the destination.

I can remember actually shaking when doing this. Then taking into account the speed of the plane and the wind speed and direction, I gave Ed an ETA at Point X (which was Faro Airport). Again he did not acknowledge whether I was right or wrong.

As I continued to fly along my planned route I was looking out for signs that I was on course and checking with the map. At one point I sighted a village which was not on my map. Oh dear! As usual I tend to talk to myself when doing things, so Ed did say at this point. "These Portuguese maps are not always up to date".

Relief. I was in the right place. As I flew on I started to see areas I knew nearer Faro and realised I had made the correct ETA. I returned to Faro and called up to join the circuit and land. Luckily I did not need to speak Portuguese as all aircraft communications internationally are in English.

The only Portuguese I can remember now, nearly 30 years later is how to order an egg sandwich, which I often did in the airport café.

***

I also flew with two other instructors while I was in Portugal, Dave Duckworth and Jeff Beardsall. Dave's wife, Jean was also an instructor and was in Faro at this time. Jean was the only woman instructor I knew. Ruth had flown with Jean quite a lot at MSF in Manchester. The next day I did two hours with Jeff Beardsall including 10 minutes of Instrument flying. This was to check out if I was on course for the next exam – the Qualifying Cross Country.

QUALIFYING CROSS COUNTRY

This is the longest flight which a student does in a P1 solo capacity before gaining a PPL. It involves flying from base to two other airfields, landing, taking off and returning to base.

In my case I flew from Faro to Sines on the coast, then from Sines to Portimao and from Portimao back to Faro. At each airfield I had to land and check in to get my form signed before moving on to the next destination. At Sines there is a small hill as you are approaching to land. This is tricky. You must have height to clear the hill, but then come down low enough to land without 'bouncing'. I did my favourite option, if not happy, go round and do it again.

When I landed and went to the club house to check in and get my form stamped, I met one of the other instructors who was with a student and he bought me a coffee. As he was going straight back to Faro he told Ed Pape he had seen me at Sines and had bought me a coffee. Ed was not pleased when I got back. He said I should have come straight back as he would worry if I was late back. However I was feeling very chilled out and enjoying myself.

My log book states:

| 28.3.92 | PA 38 | GBGSI | P1 | Faro – Sines |
| 08.55 – 10.10 | | | 1.15 | |

| 28.3.92 | PA 38 | GBGSI | P1 | Sines – Portimao |
| 10.45 – 11.45 | | | 1.00 | |

| 28.3.92 | PA 38 | GBGSI | P1 | Portimao – Faro |
| 12.10 – 12.50 | | | 0.40 | |

Qualifying Cross Country.

I remember feeling quite confident and was enjoying flying on my own. I was rash enough to take a photo when I was returning over the Santa Clara Dam, showing my dashboard settings – wings level, 90 knots, 2.5 thousand feet.

So it was quite an exciting morning. Ed then sat down with me and checked my logbook to make sure I had the hours and exercises necessary to complete my PPL. I needed some more solo time, so after a 15 minute check out in Sierra India, I was off again. Ed told me I needed 2 more solo hours so I was to fly down the coast in a westerly direction towards the junction with the Atlantic coast at Cape St Vincent. There is a lighthouse at the end of this coastline which was known as the 'last paving stone of Europe' in Columbus's time.

This was great fun. No navigation needed just following the coastline in lovely clear weather. After an hour, I turned round and flew back to Faro logging another 2.05 hours of P1 time.

By this time it was 17.05 and I had flown for over five hours during the day. I was due to return home the next day on a commercial flight. I only had one last test to do which was the GFT (General Flight Test).

I was quite worried about this. I think my flight home was at 10.30 on 29th March 92.

Ed was very chilled about the situation. Provided the weather was good, I would pack up and bring my luggage to the airport in the morning. He must have collected me very early as my log shows that we took off at 06.40 and landed at 08.20. So after 1.40 hours of being tested on everything I had learnt, we landed and he congratulated me.

What a relief. We completed paperwork. My logbook was stamped and signed "GFT Satisfactory"

I could then relax on my flight back to Manchester although I was on a high for several days after that.

CHAPTER 7

PPL AND BEYOND

So now I was at home again after a wonderful week of flying and achieving the goal I had set out to accomplish.

I was literally down to earth and was now starting to realise how much I had enjoyed being on my own. My independence and confidence were growing.

***

Although this book is not about my marriage, there were changes in my personal life during the period I am writing about, so I include some background.

As I had married in 1966 this was a marriage which may seem rather 'old fashioned' to many readers today. I was aged 19 in 1966 when the age of majority was 21, so I could not sign contracts. Chris who was 21 bought the house in his name. I had to get my parents' permission to marry.

I did not have my own bank account. Our bank accounts and finances were joint. This effectively meant I had no money to call my own.

By 1992 our daughters had left home and were leading their own lives. They were students and had jobs, finances and credit cards. Times had changed and young people were much more independent than I was in the 1960s. I had put my own needs aside to look after my family and prioritize their needs. Probably a bit of a DOOR MAT, but this was the example of married life I had from my own parents.

In the 1950s women mostly stayed at home and didn't have jobs. When WW2 ended in 1945 troops came home and wanted to return to the jobs they held before they enlisted. However many women worked in essential jobs during the war years, factories, farming and as ambulance drivers so now the government encouraged them to return to housework and looking after children.

I only started to realise this when Sam and Melanie had left home and I was still in a controlled situation. This was not always the case. When we first married things were fairly relaxed in our hippy, ex-student lifestyle. However after five years of marriage when Sam was two and I was pregnant with Melanie, Chris had an affair. He travelled a lot with his job so was often away from home.

I suppose it was inevitable that the attractions of

being away from home on business was a contrast to the young family and pregnant wife situation. When Chris told me about the affair, I was naturally upset and went to see my mother. She said this was 'normal'. My father had had affairs for years and I should simply accept it. I was shocked and horrified by this. OK, I was very naïve and had not realised that the women who sometimes came on holidays with us were actually my father's mistresses.

I was appalled by the way he treated my mother and very saddened for her.

But I would not accept this situation. I did not want to share my husband with another woman, so I told Chris he had to decide – her or me. After many discussions and re-thinking, he moved out and went into rented accommodation with the new woman.

The positive side to this was that my friend Judy moved in with me. We had lots of space and Judy was then living with her parents after her marriage had broken down. She was working full time and had a four year old daughter, Lisa.

Although I was now a single mother who was pregnant and had a two year old, Judy and I worked out a satisfactory living situation as she went to work and I looked after the children, taking Lisa to school, Sam to play group and getting lifts to my antenatal classes with Judy's boyfriend. Housework was shared. It certainly helped to keep my spirits up at a very depressing time for me.

Chris and I kept in touch and he took Sam out at weekends but after a few weeks he decided he had made a mistake and wished to return.

I was now faced with a big decision. Chris knew what he wanted. I was not so sure. Chris had said that he would go abroad if I did not have him back. OK, maybe a threat, but it needed to be taken seriously. After much discussion I decided to have him back. There were several reasons for this.

1. He was the father of my children.

2. I did not have or want another man to live with.

3. I was not working and did not want to work with two children under the age of three.

4. I did not want to claim benefits, which were not generous at this time and had no other means of earning any income.

So Chris returned, Judy and Lisa stayed on with us, Melanie was born and life settled down in a way, although it took some time to return to 'normality'. In reality it was impossible to go back to the previous situation.

During this interlude it had become clear to Chris that he wanted to stay in the family relationship. He realised he had made a mistake in leaving us and so returned. Unfortunately he then became rather possessive and controlling as he realised that if he could leave then so could I, so tried to prevent this.

***

When I returned to Manchester, my logbook had to be sent to CAA (Civil Aviation Authority) to be certified with my PPL.

It was returned with a stamp stating that I was now licensed to act as a Pilot in command (P1) or co-pilot (P2) on Group A aircraft, which are single engine planes. The certificate was valid for thirteen months from the date of test.

I also received a paper licence in a folder which holds all my certificates and current medical.

After that period I would be required to present my log book at Barton to have my entries checked and a Certificate of Experience entered and signed by one of the CAA instructors.

It has always amazed me that the driving test does not have any further requirements or time period.

If someone does not drive for years after passing a driving test they are still legally allowed to get behind a wheel of a car.

You could argue that there is more potential to harm others when flying a plane, but if you look at most light aircraft crashes the people injured or killed are usually only the pilot and passengers in the plane, whereas a driver can cause multiple pile ups on a crowded motorway especially in bad weather!

I next flew at Barton on the 28th April 92. Before I could take a club plane out on my own I had a check out with an instructor for 20 minutes, noted in my log as P1 US (pilot in command under supervision) and then took Chris for my first flight as P1 with a passenger from Barton.

This was a great milestone for me. I was now allowed to book a club plane and fly either by myself or with a friend. The aircraft I was flying at this time were Cessna 150 and 152s. These are two-seater training aircraft. The club also owned some Cessna 172s which were larger four-seater planes.

I did have a check out on a 172 with Mon Makan at this time and also did some circuits to adapt to the larger aircraft. However I was mostly flying C152s either on my own or with friends. I took my father up for a flight in June. I started flying with Ruth who had been training with me at MSF in Manchester Airport.

Ruth already had her PPL. She had stayed at Manchester Airport flying with MSF Aviation. Although Ed Pape had formed MSF Aviation Algarve there was still a club at Manchester. However this was on borrowed time as approval for a second runway at Manchester Airport was given in 1997 and work started soon afterwards. This meant that the flying clubs and other businesses on the 'South Side' would have to leave.

There were a lot of protests from local people and National agitators who lived in trees in the woods around the airport, but eventually the second runway opened in February 2001.

Flying in club planes was expensive, so I wanted to get together with like-minded people in a similar position. I wrote an advert and put it on the club noticeboard.

RECENTLY QUALIFIED PPL

SEEKS SIMILAR FOR

REGULAR FLYING TRIPS

SHARED COSTS

This advert produced some responses. All chaps (of course) as the only other woman pilot I knew was Ruth and I was already flying with her. We flew to Blackpool together in June which was an easy distance and a good day out. I was trying to persuade Ruth she really needed to change to flying out of Barton. Although she came with me, I was doing all the flying (and covering all the costs) as Ruth would need to have instruction and a type conversion on the Cessna 150s and 152s before flying as P1 at Barton.

A couple of chaps came to meet me at the club house and even came flying with me, but we didn't manage to arrange anything regular. One of them apologized and said that his wife was not happy about him flying with a WOMAN.

However I received a call from Mike Bond which was really useful for me.

At the time that Mike contacted me he had a share in an older Cessna 172, G-ARIV. He was progressing towards achieving a CPL (Commercial Pilot's Licence) and needed 700 hours to start the commercial training. Mike said I could fly the plane whenever I wanted but the deal was that I paid £15 per hour, which was effectively the fuel costs, and that he would log the hours. That suited me fine. I did not need the hours in my logbook, I was never going to go commercial, but just needed the experience.

We then flew together on a regular basis as Mike had his own business so could be flexible on times for flying. Mike is a very experienced pilot also a champion glider pilot. He is a very hardworking, positive, practical and determined person. Mike used the plane for transport trips he needed to do, so a whole new world of flights was possible for me going further distances.

Mike and I were from very different backgrounds. He is working on writing his autobiography. The part I have read about his childhood is fascinating. Mike never minced his words. He always spoke very directly.

When I was first introduced to India Victor, he said, "this is a man's plane, girl, you can't start it."

This was because it was not an electric start but a pull start which required strength. Of course he knew that this would be like a 'red rag to a bull' because I was now determined to start it myself. So with 'all four feet' on the dash board, I pulled as hard as I could and managed to start the plane.

We often used to have a cup of tea in the Barton club house after flying, but one day Mike said

"I'm going for a curry, do you want to come?"

"No I'm sorry, Mike I can't – you see I'm married".

Mike laughed and said, "Well I'm married too, but I can still eat curry!"

Oh dear. I laughed too and realised what a foolish thing I had said. Of course it made me rethink my situation. I meant that I was married to a possessive man who wouldn't want me to go out for a meal with a MAN. Not everyone lived in the same sort of situation.

As Chris and I had our own business, my working hours were flexible so I could take time off for trips in the plane. Not all these trips were logged in my logbook.

Mike would sometimes contact me to see if I could go on a flight with him. He once needed to fly to Bournemouth. I was to plan the flight from Barton to Bournemouth and return via Exeter and Welshpool. This required a lot of planning to include the route and headings as well as the radio frequencies to contact and the weather forecast. He constantly pushed me to do more instrument flying and would often cover up the instruments in the plane so that I was forced to fly without the use of these.

Mike had lots of friends who were pilots. I once flew overnight with him and his friend, Alan Yardsley. Alan had a job flying the cheques to Dublin overnight for one of the Irish banks. We flew in a Partenavia P68 from Manchester to East Midlands where we collected the bags full of cheques and cleared customs before flying to Dublin. On the way there I sat in the back, with

Alan and Mike in the front seats. I had headphones so that I could hear their conversation. Mike told jokes for most of the way. He is excellent at telling jokes and could imitate voices very well. On the way back from East Midlands I was in the front with Alan, flying as P1 US (under supervision). It was tiring flying regularly overnight so Alan was pleased to have some company which kept everyone awake.

This was now October 92 and I had done a '172 conversion' test with my previous instructor Mon Makan, so now officially allowed to fly either G-ARIV or the club 172 G-BNTP.

***

However my personal situation was no better. Since my trip to Portugal when I had realised how much I enjoyed being on my own I struggled with my married situation, but I felt I was stuck with it. Chris and I ran a business together which we owned jointly. How could I change that?

Also I did not have any one else and really just wanted to live on my own. How could I tell Chris that? I came from a background where everyone was a COUPLE. At this point in my life I don't think I knew anyone who lived on their own. Of course lots of people did live happily in a single state, but it was not a world which I had come across.

Although I wanted to leave the marriage, I didn't want to hurt Chris. This may seem odd, but we had been through a lot together with having children and running a business. We did get on well in a business sense.

The problem with marriage in Western society is that it has become focussed on a couple relationship rather than the larger family unit which still exists in some societies. This throws everything onto the expectations of the relationship. Your partner is expected to be everything – lover, parent, companion, friend, breadwinner, with very little, if any, help from a wider family group.

The family group has often reduced to the standard 'two parents and two children' model as ours had. I accept that not all marriages are the same, but it can be difficult if not impossible to change a marriage relationship after 26 years together.

As I tried to spread my wings (!) my situation became more difficult. It took me two years to have the courage to tell Chris I wanted to leave.

CHAPTER 8

G-BNTP

Around the end of 1992 I was considering buying a share in a plane at Barton myself. It was great to fly India Victor with Mike but as it was a group-share plane I could only do that when the plane and Mike were available, as I didn't own a share.

However Mike was not happy with the India Victor group. The members were not all getting on well. They had one member who took the plane to Ireland and then found that the weather was not good enough for him to fly it back to Barton. He needed to get back for work so took a commercial flight back leaving India Victor in Dublin. Of course this was very annoying for the other group members who couldn't fly the plane until someone went over to get it. As with sailing in a crew it is really important that everyone gets on with the people in the group when sharing a plane. If the situation works, it is the best and cheapest way to fly.

Mike had found out that G-BNTP was going to be sold. He suggested that we should buy the plane between us and then sell two or three other shares so that we could decide who we had in the group. So at the beginning of 1993 Mike did some negotiations and we managed to buy Tango Papa between us.

Mike was as usual a straight-talking guy. When I asked him whether it would affect his 'street cred' to buy a plane with a WOMAN. He only said, "you're not a WOMAN, you're a mate with boobs," which I guess was a compliment! We then spent some weeks getting other members for the group. If I found anyone who was interested they had to do a check-out flight with Mike. I remember one guy who seemed fine to me but Mike turned him down after a check-out flight.

The one person we both wanted was Ruth. She was a very good pilot and it would balance out the group well to have two women in it. Luckily Ruth was happy to buy in to Tango Papa. We often went flying together. We would decide on a destination airfield and plan the trip. One of us would fly there and the other would fly back. Of course as the planes are all dual control there was always someone to help if necessary. The pilot who was in control would always be in the left-hand seat. I think it would have been quite difficult to fly from the right-hand seat position due to the position of the instruments.

Ruth and I agreed to meet fairly regularly at Barton and if the weather was good we would fly, if not we would just meet for coffee and conversation. I remember once another club member (male) asking us if we were going flying and we said we weren't as we didn't like the weather. He said we were 'wimps'. However I replied that at least we were 'alive wimps'.

I would spend a lot of time in my office at work looking out of the window and peering at the sky to see what the weather was like and whether it was suitable for flying.

The other club member we invited into the group was Ted Heath (not the politician). I had known Ted for some time as a customer in our mobile communications business. He was an engineer and ran a business called M&H Plant Hire. He loved flying and was pleased to buy a share. He agreed entirely with the view that you did not fly unless the conditions were right. He was also very useful in having an office in a tall building in Stretford where he could see for miles in all directions. If doubtful about the weather you could phone Ted and ask him what he could see. If he was not busy you would hear the creak of the office chair as he leaned back, relaxed and started to talk about flying.

As I had more time than the others and, being a Capricorn liked the organisational side of things, I managed the bookings and accounts for the plane. This was not very onerous with only four of us. We kept an aeroplane log in Tango Papa where you entered the hours you flew. At the end of the month I added up the hours and sent everyone a bill. The money would be paid into the aeroplane account so that some funds would be available for maintenance checks.

As Mike had previous experience of flying groups, we went with the model which had worked with India Victor. We paid monthly for our flying hours which then covered fuel costs. There was a strict schedule of maintenance with the CAA for private planes. This included 50 hour checks and annual maintenance checks. The costs of these checks varied depending on the work needed, so we waited until we got the bill and then divided it up between us. Mike had told us there were some groups who levied a large amount every month so that they would have money in the account for the maintenance checks. Because we knew each other well, we preferred to keep the money in our own accounts and simply spilt the bills. Problems could arise if someone wanted to sell their group share and there was a large amount of money in the plane account. Barton had its own maintenance section in one of the hangars at the airfield so we only needed to book in when work was needed.

CHAPTER 9

IMC RATING

IMC stands for Instrument Meterological Conditions. This is a basic instrument rating for private pilots. Commercial pilots do an IR rating which is very different as a lot of commercial flying is spent flying on instruments, whereas a PPL would hope not to get into cloud and poor visibility.

I was certainly encouraged by Mike to do the IMC rating and I felt it would make me a safer pilot if I ever got into bad weather conditions.

An IMC Rating permits you to fly in a wider range of weather conditions, such as cloud and poor visibility. Obtaining your IMC is a great way of building up your pilot experience and, due to the UK's poor weather, it's likely to double your potential flying time.

- *Along with an instructor inside a dual controlled aeroplane, you'll need to perform at least 15 hours of instrument flying as 'Pilot under Training'*

- *Up to 5 hours of this training is completed in an EASA-STD device (Flight Simulation Training Device)*

- *Up to 2 hours of this training is completed in other FSTD's (Flight Simulation Training Device)*

- *At least 10 hours of flying is solely focused on instruments*

N.B. This is the current list of training needed, however when I did my IMC rating there was no requirement to use FSTDs probably because flying schools did not have them.

- ***Theoretical Knowledge Examinations***

- *You must pass a written theoretical knowledge examination covering subjects drawn from the IMC Rating course syllabus and the PPL (A) syllabus*

- *It includes questions on the planning & execution of a typical flight under IFR (Instrument Flight Rules) outside the controlled airspace*

Flight Test

You must complete the training before taking a Flight Test. This is conducted by a CAA examiner.

The test includes:

- *Full and limited panel instrument flying*

- *Instrument approach procedures*

- *Bad weather circuits & landings*

- *Use of radio navigation aids whilst flying by sole reference to instruments*

Completing the training and test would take about five days. So now that I owned a group share in Tango Papa I was able to book the plane for the number of days I needed to do the training and complete the course.

The instructor I had at Barton was Martin Rushbrooke who was a senior CAA instructor. He was an excellent instructor and a very gentle man. He never shouted or pushed a student but just encouraged and taught well. Although I do remember him being in despair about one of his students who never seemed to progress. He said to me once, "if you hear a gunshot coming from the Gents in the Club House, you will know that X has got his PPL so my life's work will be done".

I started flying every day with Martin from 15.3.93 – 19.3.93. We did two or three sessions in a day as instrument flying is very tiring so concentration will start to lag after an hour or so. Martin would sense when I was tired and we would land, go for coffee and start again after a break.

ILS procedures were carried out at Warton aerodrome, which is operated by BAE systems and is 6 nautical miles (nm) west of Preston. This was the hardest part of the course. ILS is the Instrument Landing System which brings all commercial aircraft in to land. The pilot will be given a heading to join up with the ILS. The pilot will report when she/he is 'established' and can therefore follow the instruments down to the landing runway. There is a cross on the instrument panel showing if you are above or below the line or to the side of the line. It is a very fine adjustment to keep the cross on the horizon and lined up in the middle.

It is easier for commercial pilots as there is a series of lights on either side of the runways at large airports, these are different colours showing if a plane is too high or too low. This system doesn't work for small light aircraft as they would always be too low on the lights system.

On 19th March 93 I took my IMC rating flight test. After an hour and twenty minutes of flying with an hour and five minutes of that spent flying on instruments, we landed and Martin told me I had passed. It was hard work but enjoyable.

As with the PPL (licence) the IMC rating is subject

to a time renewal. This time after 2 years, so I was tested and my licence renewed in March 95 and March 97.

***

On 25th March 1993 there was one of the rare occasions where life and flying clashed together. I had booked Tango Papa out and intended to fly up to Walney Island, Barrow up on the Cumbria coast, a small airfield operated by BAE Systems. It was a lovely trip up the coast followed by crossing the sea at Morecambe Bay. In order to comply with regulations I would need to cross the bay at around 3,000 feet, so that if I had an engine failure I could 'glide clear' of the sea and hopefully land somewhere safely on the land.

Chris had intended to come with me. However on the morning of the trip we were in the office and there was a staff problem which meant a serious dismissal was needed immediately. When we had dealt with the situation, Chris said that he wouldn't come on the flight, he didn't feel settled and decided he should stay in the office.

I asked if he minded if I went. He didn't. So I went

off on my own on one of the longest solo trips I had done apart from flying tests. I note from my logbook that it was an hour's flying to get there but only 45 minutes coming back to Barton. There was probably a strong northerly wind.

Over April, May and June of 93, I flew to more places with more passengers than before. When the weather was good and the nights were lighter we could fly into the evenings. The latest landing I noted when returning to Barton was 20.10. I flew to Halfpenny Green, Crosland Moor (Huddersfield), Sherburn in Elmet (Yorkshire) Swansea and Haydock Park (Southport).

This last trip was to go to a Plant Exhibition at the Haydock Park Racecourse. It was strictly PPR (prior permission required) and could be used on race days only when horses were not in sight. The Pooleys Guide shows the racetrack and an 800m east/west grass strip inside the course. The information in the Pooleys Flight Guide states that care should be taken over rough ground particularly at the end of the runways.

CHAPTER 10

TRIP TO BEVERLEY

Our younger daughter Melanie was studying for a fine arts degree in Hull over this period and in June of 1993 she had her Degree Show at Hull School of Art. Chris and I were invited to go. We wondered if it would be possible to fly over in Tango Papa, so I checked the aviation charts to see where the nearest airfields were.

There was a small grass strip north of Beverley at Linley Hill. Melanie knew where it was and would be able to drive out and collect us. I phoned to check it was all right for us to fly in on 28th June and park overnight returning to Barton on 29th June.

We went down to Barton after work and I checked out the plane. TP had just been in to the maintenance hangar at Barton so should be in good condition. When I opened the bonnet and checked the oil supply, I had difficulty undoing the cap. This was always an annoying situation. Someone in the hangar had obviously checked the oil and tightened up the cap which was now more than 'finger tight' - luckily Chris managed to undo it. I thought the oil looked rather full but was not going to be able to do anything about it right now. We taxied over to the runway and after clearance rolled down the runway and took off just before 18.00. It was a lovely summer's evening and rather warm.

The flight took just over an hour – much better than 3 hours in heavy traffic down the M62. However as we flew eastwards I was constantly doing my checks and noticed that the engine temperature was rather on the hot side. I was somewhat concerned but thought that I would just keep an eye on it during the flight. Chris was always very good in these situations. He was respectful of the fact that I was the pilot. He would help with the navigation having the aviation chart on his lap but did not interfere with my job.

At one point the operator on the radio frequency we were talking to asked me for my position. Although I had a GPS and therefore knew exactly where we were on the map, the operator wanted to know a PLACE NAME. I can remember saying, "stand by, I'll call you back", while we frantically searched the map for somewhere which had a name and wasn't just a field in the middle of the countryside! After this trip Chris got me an extra piece of equipment which gave more useful details from the GPS fix like '2 nm ESE of X'. This obviously kept the radio operators very happy.

When nearing Beverley we called up for permission to land and park up for the night. The airfield was simply a farmer's field and was very casual and friendly. It was operated by Hull Aero Club.

Melanie had been driving down a small lane to the air strip and saw the plane coming in so by the time we had tied down and checked in she was ready to take us into Hull for the evening. I remember the degree show well. Although I like art I was really not up to speed with some of the student's displays, one of them was a pile of sugar and another was some rotting fruit. I did comment that I had some of that in my kitchen at home! Melanie had used old fashioned underwear, corsets, etc. and dyed the garments in natural home- made dyes. It was very effective and made an interesting art display.

The next morning Melanie drove us back to the airstrip and brought her friend, Ki with her. Both Melanie and Ki wanted to have a flight in Tango Papa, so I took them for a short wizz around the local area before bringing them back and preparing to fly back to Manchester with Chris.

The airstrip was very quiet. When I asked in the tower which runway they were using that morning, I was told to taxi down to the air sock and then make a decision and let them know which I preferred! The options were 12 or 30 (each end of the grass runway).

The trip back to Barton was uneventful. Luckily the engine temperature had settled back to normal. I think it had just been a combination of a hot summer's evening and a full oil supply, but I am a very good worrier and so can worry about all sorts of things which are probably unnecessary.

CHAPTER 11

TRIP TO SCOTLAND

Although by this time I had done quite a lot of local flying on my own or with friends, I had not undertaken a longer trip without a more experienced pilot.

Mike had often talked about the island of Gigha which was off the west coast of Scotland. He encouraged me to fly up there.

I got out my aviation chart and Pooleys Flight Guide and had a look. It certainly looked interesting and challenging. Gigha has a grass runway 07/25 of 720m in length. It is unmanned and unlicensed. (Airfields that are unlicensed cannot be used for commercial flights). It has no radio but pilots can contact RAF Machrihanish for weather information. It was PPR (prior permission required) if you wanted to land there. Pooleys Guide states that the landing fee is £15 but there is a £5 discount if you stay overnight at the Gigha Hotel. This was useful as there was only one hotel on the island so we would stay there anyway. It also states that aircraft should avoid overflying the village on Sundays between 1200 and 1300.

RAF Machrihanish is 3.5 miles west of Campbeltown at the tip of the Kintyre Peninsula. There have been two airfields at Machrihanish. The first was constructed during the First World War and was used by the RAF and Royal Naval Air Service. It closed when a second airfield was built in the Second World War and used by the Fleet Air Arm.

During the 1960s the airfield was redeveloped and became RAF Machrihanish. It was used by the US Navy during the Cold War and also became a base for the US Navy SEALs.

***

Having decided to take a trip north of the border into Scotland I booked the plane out for a week and planned the venture. Chris would come with me. We would fly to Gigha first, stay overnight and then go north to Aberdeen to stay with our friends, Max and Grace who were living there. We had known them well when they lived in Didsbury but Max was now the Vice Chancellor of Aberdeen University so we did not get many opportunities to see them.

When Max and Grace had first moved to Aberdeen they invited a group of Manchester friends to a Burns Night celebration at their new residence which was a palatial house in the city. They hired a minibus to take us there. The bus would depart on a Friday evening from the clock tower in Didsbury village. Rumours spread around Didsbury. Nobody liked to ask if you were invited in case you were not, likewise we did not like to say we had been invited as maybe the people we were talking to had not.

Eventually the evening arrived and the minibus departed with a good stock of champagne and glasses for the trip provided by Max. The party of people was very distinguished, consisting of academics, solicitors, lawyers, etc. Chris and I are not in any way academic but were probably the only business owners in the gathering.

On arrival in Aberdeen at the Vice Chancellor's house we were met by Max and Grace and rooms were allocated. Although it was a very large house the rooms varied enormously from the posh guest rooms to the small attic rooms. The system of allocation was very fair so that no-one felt upset. Room numbers were on folded pieces of paper and were picked from a hat. Chris and I had an attic room, but as the hospitality over the weekend was excellent we did not mind as not much time was spent in rooms.

The Burns Night supper on Saturday night was an amazing evening. I had never attended a Burns Night (even though my grandfather was Scottish) so had to be briefed on the proceedings. The food was haggis, tatties and neeps (this is Scottish for haggis, potatoes and mashed swede). The only alcohol served was whisky.

Fortunately I like whisky but Chris only drank white wine. He had been forewarned about the situation so had brought a bottle (actually several) with him. I decided I would need to pace myself on the drinking front in order to survive the evening without getting very drunk.

Because no-one was supposed to be drinking anything except whisky, Chris kept his wine bottle under the table which fortunately had large white tablecloths. When he wanted to refill his glass he would bend down and fill it under the table in a discrete manner. After a while the lady sitting next to him asked what he was doing. When she discovered he had a bottle of white wine she asked if she could have some. She didn't like whisky either.

A traditional Burns Night supper takes place on the nearest date possible to 25th January which was the day Robert (Rabbie) Burns was born. Apart from the traditional food and drink there are speeches. I don't remember them all but there was a toast to the haggis which was piped in. After the food there were speeches including one to 'the Old Enemy' i.e. the English. There was a reply from one of our group from south of the border. Of course the company consisted of many people who were very erudite and accomplished at making speeches in the course of their jobs, so the speeches were excellent and very amusing.

Having survived a very enjoyable evening we returned to Didsbury in the minibus on Sunday but did not drink champagne on the way back, as most people were sleeping.

***

We left Barton on 3.10.93 intending to go straight to Gigha for the first night. We had phoned for the weather situation and although it looked okay before we left, as we flew north the visibility over the coast was deteriorating. To get to Gigha we would have to fly over some fairly high hills on the Scottish mainland so as I am a very careful pilot I decided that we would go to Carlisle for the first night. We could divert in along the Solway Firth. It was an easy route to follow even in bad visibility. Chris and I owned an old mill house in Cumbria south of Carlisle so we would get a taxi from the airport and stay there for the night. This was a very safe plan. We would be able to set off earlier the next day if the weather was good.

The weather the next day was much better, clear over the hills. We set off back to Carlisle, checked out Tango Papa and set off up to Gigha. I had already called the hotel owner to book in for the night. He said that as the airstrip was in the south of the island, and did not have mobile phone coverage, he requested that we circle the hotel and waggle the wings. He would then come down to the airfield and collect us by car.

It was a good flight via Lockerbie and Wigton. One hour and 55 minutes flying time. As we came over Gigha we saw the airstrip at the south of the island, then flew over a very large house surrounded by woods and gardens in the centre of the island. This must be the hotel. I did a slow circuit over the building and flew back to land and tie down Tango Papa safely for the night.

I was a bit worried that this looked like a posh hotel. I hadn't brought any smart clothes with me, but I needn't have worried. We were still awaiting collection after we had tied down and removed a bag and valuables for the night, so we attempted to phone the hotel. I managed to get a signal and got a call through to the hotel manager. He said he hadn't seen us fly in so would come to get us now.

Gigha is Old Norse for God's Island. It is part of Argyll and Bute. The island is very green with a mild climate, higher than average sunshine hours and fertile soil. The main settlement is Ardminish. It has been continuously inhabited since Norse times. It is the ancestral home of the Clan MacNeill but was subsequently sold to James Williams Scarlett in 1865 whose son built the Mansion House of Achamore and owned the island of Gigha until 1919.

Various people had owned Gigha including Sir James Horlick who made the gardens at Achamore.

By the 1960s the population was down to 163. The private landlords who owned the island had not always had the islander's interests at heart. So eventually in March 2002 there was a buy-out by the local population funded by Lottery and Heritage funding to create the Isle of Gigha Heritage Trust.

The manager chatted as we drove north past the big house in gardens and woods which turned out to be the Mansion House of Achamore and not

the island's hotel. We stayed quiet at this point
not admitting to our mistake. The hotel was small
and there were very few people in the bar. Chris
and I had a drink there and an elderly Scottish
gentleman engaged us (or rather I should say,
Chris) in conversation. He seemed to completely
ignore me.

*I had come across this situation before when we
were on holiday in Sri Lanka many years earlier.
Chris and I took a taxi to Candy in the hills which
had been General Mountbattan's headquarters
during WW2. Our daughters preferred to stay by
the pool at the hotel, so because of this we only
went for the day. The taxi driver kept talking to
Chris, ignoring me and wanted to know where his
sons were. Chris explained that we didn't have
any sons, only daughters. The taxi driver kept
forgetting this and coming back to questions about
our sons. He also kept telling us that, "100% of
people stay overnight in Candy", clearly ignoring
the fact that we were not!*

The Scottish gentleman asked Chris how we got
to the island. Chris explained that we had flown in
and our plane was at the airstrip, also that I was the
pilot. The gentleman did not believe this. He was

so insistent about this that I almost expected him to come to the strip and watch me take off in the morning! Clearly women were incapable of such things.

I have to say that I did not sleep well that night. It was quite scary being on such a small island knowing that the only way we would get out of there was by me flying. The airstrip was simply a grass field. There were no other planes and no service hangars, control towers or radio service. Added to that was the fact that there was a small slope on the runway so we would need to be taking off downhill rather than uphill. I dreaded the wind being in the wrong direction and not being able to take off until the wind changed.

Luckily on this occasion the worry was unnecessary. The morning was clear and bright, the wind was in the right direction and having been dropped at the airfield we untied the plane, I did the checks and took off. Phew!

In order to fly on to Aberdeen we would need to refuel. I had planned to do this at Glasgow airport, but Glasgow was low lying, inland and in mist, so not accessible for a light aircraft on a VFR flight. I made the decision to refuel at Prestwick. I note that it is now known as Glasgow Prestwick airport. It has an enormous runway of 2987m which was very different from the Gigha strip of 720m which we had departed from. It is right on the coast so not as affected by the weather as the inland airports. Although a big international airport, it is the fifth busiest airport in Scotland after Glasgow, Edinburgh, Aberdeen and Inverness. I think it was built to take increased international flights to Scotland. Passenger numbers peaked in 2007 to 2.4 million following a decade of rapid growth but then declined as low-cost carriers lost business.

At the time I went there it was fairly deserted. I must have been keen to get out of Gigha as my logbook shows that I took off at 09.35 and landed at 10.15 in Prestwick. I called up the airport on their approach frequency requesting landing for refuelling. I was told to come straight in as there were no other aircraft in the circuit. I was then asked to expedite as we were number one to land. I couldn't go any faster! It seemed to take an awful long time to get down the approach and onto the runway. On landing, a Land Rover came out to meet us and we were requested to follow it, which was a good thing as the airport is very large and we could have been taxiing all over the place to find the fuel. The staff were very friendly and chatted to me while they refuelled Tango Papa. I didn't have to climb up on the wings and put the fuel in myself unlike the situation at small airports.

At 11.30 we were on our way in clear weather although avoiding Glasgow which was still in mist, we flew up to Aberdeen via Loch Lomond and Perth then up the east coast. The flying time was just over 2 hours.

***

Since the discovery of North Sea Oil off the coast of Aberdeen in the 1970s the city has been known as the off shore oil capital of Europe. Aberdeen's buildings incorporate locally quarried grey granite which sparkles in the sun due to its high mica content giving the city its name as the Granite City. The city has a long sandy coastline with a marine climate giving cool summers and mild winters.

Aberdeen Airport is located 5nm NW of Aberdeen in the suburb of Dyce. It is the main heliport for the offshore North Sea Oil and Gas industry. There is one passenger terminal and four helicopter terminals. Helicopters account for nearly half of all aircraft movements.

After landing at this busy airport we contacted our friends, Grace and Max. Grace was in Manchester at the time so Max came to collect us. I'm not sure how long we had intended to stay with them, but it did turn out to be longer than we had expected.

I had decided that I would make the flight back to Barton in one leg. There wasn't anywhere else I wanted to go and I just felt I needed to get home. In order to do this I had to make sure that the weather would be good for VFR flight not only in Scotland but down as far as Manchester. I phoned the local flight weather centre to check the situation.

The first day I rang, requesting a weather report for a single engine VFR flight from Aberdeen to Barton, the operator said I had no chance that day and probably not the following day either, but he advised me to phone and check anyway.

I phoned, there was no possibility. The last thing I wanted was to start south from Aberdeen and run into bad weather over the Lake District Mountains with nowhere to land. However the operator (the same guy, who I was now getting to know) said there may be a window of clear weather in the middle of the day on the following day. He said that I should get down to the airport and phone him from there for a final check before departing.

The next morning Chris and I packed and got a lift to the airport. I phoned the weather centre. My (by now) friend was optimistic but said that we must leave urgently at midday. There was a weather window but another weather front was moving north bringing low cloud and rain into the Manchester area, so delay was not advised.

Aberdeen is a large international airport. In order to get out to Tango Papa who was waiting patiently on the apron, we had to go through the usual sort of security checks you will be familiar with when going on holiday. We tried to stay calm as we queued to go through baggage checks.

The staff did not understand my situation even though I explained I owned a plane on the tarmac and needed to get out to it. We had some baggage with us and I had my flight bag and a tool kit in a large toolbox. The ground staff man who was putting the bags through was becoming a bit exasperated with me. "Where do you think you are going to put that toolbox?" He asked. "On the back seat", I answered calmly.

We did manage to get through to the air side, get the checks done and request taxi for take-off by about midday. My log records that we took off at 12.15. Phew!

We flew in on 5th October 1993 and finally flew out on 8th October.

***

So after take-off I flew south first of all down the east coast of Scotland via Edinburgh and then inland to pass Carlisle.

I am very familiar with the route south down the M6 from Carlisle back to Manchester. When you are following a feature line on the ground, e.g. a road or river, aviation law states that you should keep the feature on your left hand side as the pilot in charge sits in the left hand seat.

By this time Chris was beginning flying training in helicopters. When he flew with another pilot friend they were flying following a railway line which was on the right side of the helicopter. Chris commented that he should have been on the other side. His friend said nobody bothered with that rule. Chris stated that as his wife did, his friend could meet her flying the other way!

So as I followed the M6 south the cloud was starting to increase and lower. The hills around Junctions 39 to 36 are fairly high, so keeping in mind the rules to be more than 500 feet from a person, object or building (unless you are in a highspeed RAF jet) I went as low as I could to stay out of cloud but keep at a legal height.

But by this time, you may remind me, that I had an IMC rating, but this was very much intended to be used for emergency situations only. No pilot willingly goes into cloud over high mountains unless it is absolutely necessary. With relief we were able to descend as the mountains give way to lower ground after Junction 36 and the coastline becomes visible at Morecambe Bay.

I now called up the weather centre at Warton to get the forecast for the Manchester area. It is always interesting how people in the same situation remember different things. Chris remembers hearing the surprise in the operator's voice when a woman's voice called in saying:

Golf Bravo November Tango Papa, Cessna 172 from Aberdeen to Barton requesting weather for the Manchester area.

The radio operator told me the cloud base was lowering at Barton, I would not be able to land there and would have to divert to Manchester.

Gulp! This was madness.

I had no intention of going into Manchester Airport.

1. Air traffic control would probably have refused to give permission for me to land.

2. There would be a large landing fee, and even if I left Tango Papa there for a short time, parking would be expensive.

3. Chris's car was at Barton.

Luckily while I was trying to find the words for a short and polite response, bearing in mind that anyone on the same frequency can hear what everyone else is saying, Martin Rushbrooke (my IMC flying instructor from Barton) came on the air.

He called up to say he was in the Barton circuit and the cloud base was high enough for me to land. So I proceeded onwards with relief. We landed at 15.19 after 3 hours and 4 minutes which was the longest flight in command that I had undertaken. I realised afterwards that Mike had never been to Gigha – he just thought it would be a good trip, which it was! It was also the last time Chris flew with me. The beginning of 1994 was the start of some very big changes in my life.

CHAPTER 12

ENGINE PROBLEMS

The next flight I did was not until 15.11.93 as Tango Papa had to go in to the maintenance hangar for his regular C of A (Certificate of Airworthiness) check.

I was the first one to fly him after this check.

Note: I always refer to TP as him. Traditionally boats are feminine, but I'm not sure about planes. We did discover in the group that the chaps would refer to TP as female whereas the women referred to him as a bloke. Strange! Must be a sex thing! Remember what Capt. Flashheart said in Blackadder "You should treat your planes like you treat your women, get into them 3 times a day and take them to heaven".

So on 15th November I flew to Caernarfon. It was one of my favourite trips. Very scenic and very easy. I took Steve, one of our young salesmen with me. He hadn't flown with me before and was very keen to go. From Barton we flew through the Liverpool zone via the VOR at Wallasey, WAL which is out on the coast. We then tracked down the Wales coast along to Caernarfon.

The small airfield is 3.5 nm SW of the town of Caernarfon which is easy to identify with its castle. It is in the vicinity of Valley MATZ a military training airfield so incoming aircraft are advised to contact them to check if they have any flights expected. The airfield is mainly used by small, fixed wing aircraft, helicopters and microlites. It has the standard triangular three runways as favoured by the RAF.

In the 2000s the airfield underwent redevelopment and expansion with a maintenance and storage centre, Visitor Centre, shop and café. It is now home to three Wales Air Ambulance helicopters.

***

Over the last few years I have been walking the Wales Coast Path in company with some walking friends. It was very exciting when we were doing the Anglesey coast path section being near Valley when the fast RAF jets came and went at very high speeds. We also visited Caernarfon Airfield which had changed a lot since I flew in there in the 1990s. Sadly our annual walking holiday has been suspended due to Coronavirus. We were about to start the Pembrokeshire section in June 2020. Hopefully we can continue with this in June 2021.

It was very windy when we came into the airfield at Caernarfon. It is right on the coast and there were some strong cross winds. I brought Tango Papa in 'crabwise' on the approach to compensate for the wind but just before we touched down I had to straighten up in order to land straight on the runway. We checked in and then went to the café for tea and cake before returning to Barton.

When I was back in the Club House at Barton I met Mike who asked me how the plane was after his service. I said it was OK apart from the throttle which was very stiff. Mike said it was because we had had new throttle bushes fitted. It was the "newness which would wear off".

I never realised until afterwards how close I came to a disaster.

Ted's Story

I was enjoying this flight, just a one hour jolly in the Barton local flying area. The aircraft had been out of service for 3 weeks for its C of A and I had not flown for about 6 weeks or so, I remember I was quite eager to get some practice in and get up and blow the cobwebs off.

Because Tango Papa had so recently come out of maintenance, I was meticulous with my ground checks, peering into every nook and cranny for missing split pins or the proverbial screwdriver or oily rag left in a corner just waiting to creep out and snag a control cable at the wrong moment, not that I didn't have complete faith in our maintenance engineers, I did, but I always think it pays to check for yourself.

So here I am about 45 minutes after take-off number 3 on finals for zero 9 North, no problems with rejoin, outside air temperature was only +2 and quite damp so lots of carb heat when I throttled back to descend dead side.

The airfield is very busy today, but then again it often is on a sunny Sunday afternoon. Number 1 has just done a touch and go but I am catching up on number 2 which is a 3 axis microlight, I think it is a Thruster, OK I tell myself I'll go round, check my height – 300 feet, call tower, check carb heat is off, full power, start to dump the flaps, it's odd I am not really climbing as much as usual and not accelerating, check the rpm 1900 showing, airspeed 70 knots. I look at the throttle – Ah! The throttle's not fully open, almost 1 inch left, I push the throttle, no movement, push harder, no movement and it feels springy, no rpm increase, check the height, 500 feet, speed 70 knots, carb ice! Can't be I have only just turned off full carb heat, I turn cross wind early over the end of the runway, check my height 600 feet, and I am not going up anymore, pushing hard on the throttle, no movement, pull and push – no movement, I check the friction nut whilst turning down wind, keep the circuit tight as I may have a problem here! Friction nut is loose, try the throttle again, I push hard and pull, I didn't really mean to pull, but I did and DISASTER. It moves with a jerk the wrong way and my meagre 1900rpm is suddenly reduced to 1200.

All is suddenly clear, the carburettor butterfly or butterfly shaft is stuck, when I try to push the throttle in, the springy feeling is the outer sheaf of the boden cable giving, when I pull it's a solid feeling with no give at all. Rpm has steadied to just about 1200, check height, still 600 feet.

My old instructor's voice suddenly comes into my head, "engine trouble in the circuit turn into field". Time for a good look out all around, lots of aircraft about, there is one ahead to my right, one on short finals, one on the runway just taking off and two or three others scattered about the circuit.

I take a moment to assess my situation, but all doubts have now gone, deep breath press the PTT button and make the call "MAY DAY, MAY DAY, MAY DAY, GOLF BRAVO NOVEMBER TANGO PAPA, THROTTLE STUCK"! That's all I get out before I realise I am three quarters the way down the runway at 400 feet, instructor's voice in my head again " AVIATE NAVIGATE COMMUNICATE". In that order.

I turn in and aim for the zero 9 numbers, check

airspeed 70 knots, that's good, I trade 10 knots of airspeed for some height. A voice in my headset.

"Golf Tango Papa your position please".

Has he spoken to me before? I can't recall, I want to unlock my door but can't let go of the control yolk because I haven't had time to trim the aircraft. I press the PTT switch.

"Downwind abeam zero 9 numbers throttle's stuck at 1200 rpm. I am turning in to the field and should be able to make a landing".

I am now thinking to myself, hope that he has got that, as I don't think it was very clear, it has gone from my mind in a second as I realise I am coming in at about 90 degrees to the runway and too high.

Full flaps straight on, no messing about, now my 1200 rpm is now too much power, would you believe it! I realise I need some control of power and so I pull the mixture control full out and listen to the note of the engine as it starts to die, I push it in again until the engine starts to pick up and then I pull it out again and so on and so on. This gives me some power control, crude I know, but it works and is better than nothing. I bank hard left power on, nose down and I am over the hedge with a full 50 feet or so of height at about 45 degrees to the runway. Mixture control full out now and cut the engine, a gentle bank left to somewhere near the zero 9 runway about a third of the way in.

I thought of, switches and fuel off, but I am in the flair and it is too late so pull back hard on the yoke and it's somehow different without the prop turning but I am down and rolling to a halt! As the rescue vehicles arrive along-side me it's odd but the first thought that sprung to mind was, "Damn it. I was enjoying this flight".

And I WAS enjoying this flight.

Definitely a Hamlet moment when I landed safely.

Ted Heath Cessna 172 Sky hawk G-BNTP
Barton Aerodrome
21-11-93

I am grateful to Ted for allowing me to insert his account of the engine failure and brilliant landing without power at Barton. Those who were watching said he did a perfect landing. Although I was not there to see it, Ted told me how he felt afterwards. After he landed the fire truck and maintenance vehicle rushed across the airfield towards him.

Tom who was head of the maintenance team climbed into the plane and asked Ted to taxi over to the Maintenance Hangar. Ted explained that he couldn't. As the throttle had stuck he couldn't get any power to taxi. So a rather annoyed (and maybe embarrassed) Tom got the tow truck and hitched up Tango Papa to be towed into Maintenance. This was not looking good as the plane had just completed its annual service.

Of course it was concluded that the throttle bushes were too tight. I was so relieved that it had been Ted flying as he was a very experienced pilot and a brilliant engineer. If I was flying on this occasion I'm sure I would not have been as quick thinking as he was. With the throttle stuck there was no option to just do a circuit while you thought out what to do or talked to someone on the radio. You needed to make a decision and take action.

Ted told me he was somewhat shaken up by the incident and when he went home he did not tell his wife, Anne, straight away but went out into the garden to calm down. He then decided to write down his account before he forgot it.

CHAPTER 13

PERSONAL PROBLEMS

The rest of November and December were not good months for weather or for me. I realised afterwards that I had been depressed. I became lethargic. I couldn't be bothered to do anything, even making a cup of tea seemed an effort. This was very unlike my normal state.

In the first week of November we had a Bonfire Party up at our Cumbria house where we went for weekends. I can remember standing round the bonfire with our neighbour, Sue. She thought I was a bit quiet and asked me how I was. I admitted to being tired and depressed and that things were not good between Chris and me. She was shocked. Trouble was everyone thought we were Mr and Mrs Perfect. We ran a successful business together, our daughters were achieving well at university and life seemed settled. As I had been brought up in the era where you didn't talk about your personal problems, I hadn't said anything to any of my friends about my dilemma. I just kept a stiff upper lip!

In fact I was deeply unhappy. While our daughters were still living at home I was busy looking after home and family life as well as running the business, but when they had gone to university,

I realised that they were now living independent adult lives whereas I was in a controlling marriage.

I had been keen to go on holiday to India at this time. I was still practicing yoga and wanted to go and see the place where it all happened. Chris did not want to go. His view was that it was a dirty, smelly place and I would get ill. I suggested that we could have separate holidays one year. I could go to India and he could go somewhere else of his choice. Chris was against this idea. He thought there was no point in being married if you had separate holidays. How much longer would I accept this situation?

***

Germaine Greer's The Female Eunuch was published in 1971. I had a copy and read it avidly. Germaine Greer challenged everything. The book was very different and shocking. If women couldn't change the world, they could start by changing themselves.

I also read Intimacy and Solitude by Stephanie Dowrick. It is a wonderful book about balancing the need for a relationship with the individual's need for space, time and solitude.

She quotes a woman who finally left her husband because she was fed up with washing his T shirts and turning them the right way out. She didn't mind the washing so much but why couldn't he turn them the right way out himself instead of just dropping them on the floor like a teenager?

Some men constantly move between the adult/child situation. Sometimes dominating and controlling their wives and sometimes expecting to be looked after as if they were a child. All I wanted was to be treated like an equal adult.

It had probably taken me two years to realise that I had to leave the marriage. Chris was not going to change so I had to, in order to survive. However I did not want to be unkind. I knew that it would be very hurtful to Chris to tell him that I wanted to leave him, not because I had anyone else but because I wanted to live on my own. That sounds a bit unpleasant to the person you are leaving.

There are many men who are not happy with life on their own. If their marriage or relationship breaks down they will quickly find someone else to live with. However women are to blame for this situation as well. The longer they go on accepting being dominated in a relationship, the longer they will be unhappy.

There was also the practical matters. We owned and ran a business 50/50. How could I get out of this? It would be very disruptive for everyone.

***

Things came to a head at Christmas that year. Chris and I would go up to Cumbria for the Christmas and New Year holiday period. Our business was hectic up until Christmas Eve when we closed at lunch time in order to drive north to Fawcett Mill.

We then started to prepare for the family who would arrive and the amount of entertaining we would do throughout this period. Beds to be made up. Shopping for food, alcohol, etc. meant a two hour round trip to either Kendal or Penrith where the nearest supermarkets were located. I was not only depressed by this time, I was exhausted. Tempers were strained, people were on edge so the escalation of the situation was probably inevitable.

Between Christmas and New Year we hosted a party. This started at lunchtime and went on until evening. Local friends called in, friends and family from further afield came and stayed, so more bed making and supermarket shopping.

When most people had left the party and those who were staying had gone to bed, I was sitting by the fire in the living room with two neighbours of ours from our home in Salford Quays. Chris had gone to bed, he had drunk a lot of wine. He was very cross as Mike had phoned me in the afternoon to report on Tango Papa. The weather was fairly wild and windy, so Mike had gone down to Barton to put some extra tie downs on the plane. Due to their very large and high wings, Cessna 172s could be vulnerable to being flipped over in strong winds. In fact India Victor did turn over and get damaged leading to a 'write off' situation. But Chris still found it difficult to accept that I had friends who were men.

So the evening was quiet and peaceful until we heard a noise upstairs. Chris had woken up still feeling cross. Some crashing and shouting followed. One friend went upstairs to talk to him. I stayed with the other. My heart was pounding, I was feeling very anxious but also in a way relieved. This was the first time our friends had been aware of the deteriorating state of our relationship. Eventually things calmed down and everyone went to bed. I moved to sleep in a spare bedroom as most people had returned to their homes leaving some rooms free. My mind was certainly in a whirl but all was now quiet in the house and eventually I managed to get to sleep.

***

The next morning Chris came into my room with a cup of tea. He sat down on the bed and apologized for his behaviour the night before. However this had happened many times before. I told him he couldn't keep shouting at me and then thinking it would be all right to say he was sorry and carry on as usual. This time things needed to change. We waited until all our visitors had departed later in the day and then sat down for a discussion. I needed some space to be on my own and think. I told Chris I wanted to leave him and live on my own for a trial period. I didn't have anyone else, I just wanted to live on my own.

We were sitting outside on the patio. Chris was feeling upset. I was feeling relieved. At last something was HAPPENING. I had taken the decision and that was the first step. Yes things would be hard, but it was a start. A bit similar to jumping out of a plane with a parachute. Just take the leap and then deal with what happens next. From that day onwards I simply had to take every day as it came and manage the problems and barriers I encountered.

CHAPTER 14

NIGHT RATING

We cleared up and packed up the house before driving back to Manchester. It was now New Year.

Life settled down a little in January 1994. Chris wrote a letter to our immediate family, parents and daughters explaining our situation. Both daughters who were at Fawcett Mill with us over Christmas had realised things were not good between us.

Chris and I realised that we couldn't continue to work together full time in the business so made plans to sell it. We had worked well with a larger company, Talkland, in the mobile phone business. Their MD, Peter had always said that if ever we wanted to retire from the business he would be interested in buying it. So Chris took a trip down to see Peter at Talkland's head office in Banbury and tell him about our situation.

Chris had obviously expected sympathy but Peter was enthusiastic. He said that when he was 50 he would leave his wife and go and live in a Greek island. When Chris asked him, who with, Peter said he didn't know but he was sure he could find someone!

Peter was keen to do a deal with us for the purchase of our business, but of course accountants got involved and 'due diligence' needed to be carried out. This needed to be done discretely. We employed about 50 people and wanted to do a deal which would be beneficial for them.

***

Life became rather stressful for both of us. The month of January 94 was an alcohol free month for me and Chris. Sam had already decided to do a dry January. This seemed a tough thing to do as Sam and her partner Dave were regular drinkers. Sam said she always went to lots of parties and social gatherings in December and was fed up with waking up in the morning and not being able to remember what she had said the night before! I told her that I had the opposite problem – I could remember what I had said and was often embarrassed by it!

This lack of alcohol helped our situation enormously. Once I had decided to do it I found it quite interesting. We went to all the usual social occasions with no 'drink drive' worries which gave a feeling of freedom. I can remember being at a friend's 50th birthday party and chatting to some friends late in the evening when I noticed that people were talking complete nonsense! It took me some time to realise that it was because everyone was drunk except me. Quite a sobering thought.

I had started to look at one bedroom flats in Manchester city centre. I didn't tell anyone I was doing this. Although our immediate family knew our situation, we did not want anyone else to know at this stage.

The first flats I looked at were in Castle Quay, a great Victorian warehouse building overlooking the canal, but unfortunately all the good one beds had been sold. I chatted to the saleswoman who asked me what I was looking for. I said I wanted a one bed flat as close to the city centre as possible. The saleswoman told me about Granby Village which had been developed by Wimpey and was selling on Whitworth Street. I went there and loved it. The complex consisted of 5 blocks, 3 old warehouse buildings and two new builds.

There was a leisure centre with swimming pool, gym and games room, also two floors of underground car parking. Wimpey were selling each building as it was completed. Venice Court, which was a new build was selling at the time I viewed the site. I had a lot of one bed flats to choose from. They were light and airy with excellent double glazing and fully carpeted throughout.

I chose one which looked out of the complex with views of the gardens, road and other buildings so I could see LIFE going on instead of the ones which looked into the inner courtyard. I arranged to reserve the flat I liked best and went away to arrange the finances. However this was not as easy as I had hoped!

***

Looking at my flying logbook I note that I flew from Blackpool to Barton with Mike, which means that he would have flown there. With two pilots we would often do a flight each to get some practice in. I hadn't flown since the end of November and was able to do 15 minutes instrument flying practice as well.

On the 17th January 94 I flew Tango Papa to Liverpool on my own and left him there. I had arranged to do my Night Rating with Ed Pape who was now back in England from Portugal and doing flight training instruction at Barton.

THE NIGHT RATING is a 5 hour course with no exams or flight tests. It qualifies Private Pilots to fly VFR at night.

The course includes:

- *at least 3 hours dual night training*

- *1 hour dual night navigation with at least one dual cross country flight of at least 50 kms*

- *5 solo take offs and full stop landings at night*

It was not possible to do a Night Rating at Barton as the airfield closed at dusk having no night lighting. Liverpool was the nearest quiet airport to be able to fly at night. There were very few flights out of there after dark, some charter flights and mail flights but generally quiet.

The airport at Liverpool is on the banks of the River Mersey 6.5nm south east of Liverpool city centre. Built in the grounds of Speke Hall it was originally called Speke Airport. Scheduled flights by Imperial Airways were started in 1930 with a service to Croydon Airport, near London via Barton (Manchester) and Castle Bromwich Aerodrome (Birmingham).

During WW2 the airport was requisitioned by the RAF and known as RAF Speke. Rootes built a factory nearby building bombers and Lockheed assembled fighter planes with parts shipped from the US to Liverpool Docks.

The City Council took over control in 1961 and

development started. A new runway of 2286 metres was opened in 1966.

In 1990 the airport was privatised and is now owned by Peel Holdings. The name was changed to Liverpool John Lennon Airport in 2001 and a new terminal was opened in 2002.

When I delivered Tango Papa there and parked him up for his stay, Ed met me by car and took me back to Manchester. Ed lived on the west side of Manchester, so it was easy to get to Liverpool and back.

We then started a regular evening run to go out to Liverpool and fly. It was a good time of year to do the Night Rating as it was dark early, so we only needed to wait until after the rush hour traffic had gone and then get out to the airport. I can't remember how far back I had booked this, but it was very good for me to have something else to take my mind off my personal situation. Ed was a good friend as well as an excellent pilot and instructor. He was also very good at telling jokes and amusing stories.

The first night we went was 19th January. We flew for two hours which included a 30 minute cross country, night familiarisation and circuits. It is very strange to fly in the dark. Roads and motorways were very easy to see and follow due to their lighting but when outside the city areas things looked very different. Buildings could just be large black shapes against bright areas.

When we had done the familiarisation we started the circuits. This meant taxiing, taking off, flying round the circuit, and coming in to land. I was a little anxious about doing this on my own, but Ed had assured me I would not be going solo yet!

He would constantly tell stories and when we got to the point of lining up to take off, he would stop the story and say he would finish it when we landed. I guess this relaxed me a lot because after a few circuits when we were taxiing down to the hold for take-off Ed told me to stop the plane as he was going to get out. I must have been feeling quite confident by now as I then flew my first solo night circuit and got back to hear the end of the last story!

We returned to Liverpool to complete the Night Rating on 30th January. It was a busy evening. I started flying at 20.35 and did another 4 solo take offs and full stop landings (not just touch and go, which can be done when first practicing circuits for daytime flights)

We then did an hour's Night Cross Country for the Navigation section. After that I did a solo Night Navigation where I was required to go over to Barton and back. It doesn't state in the above information I got off the Internet that a student is required to do a solo cross country. Maybe things have changed or maybe Ed just thought I should do one. Who knows?

So at the end of the evening, my log book was stamped and signed by Ed certifying my entries for Night Flying. Of course I had to send off my Log Book to the CAA to get the Certificate of my Night Rating.

During this evening lots of questions came up about night flying. I remember that I was asked what I would do if I had an engine failure at night? The answer was that you should head for an area which was dark in the hope that it was an open field area where you could get the plane down.

But what would happen if it wasn't? Ed said that as you got near the dark area you should turn on your landing lights to see what was there. But supposing you found that the dark area was in fact an area of buildings with no lights on, or a forest or even a lake? All difficult if not impossible to make a good landing site.

So what would you do then? The answer I was told was to turn the landing lights off!!!!

***

I made an offer on the flat in Venice Court and set about trying to organise a mortgage. Chris was not keen for me to buy a flat. He thought I should rent one.

Our neighbours at Salford Quays were very helpful and supportive. Sandra worked for a finance company and said she could arrange a mortgage for me. So I filled in all the forms and waited. The results came back after a search to reveal that I had a joint mortgage with Chris on our Salford Quays house. I explained that he would be remaining in the property and I would be buying the new flat for me to live in due to our separation. This explanation was accepted but the mortgage company wanted Chris to sign a form agreeing that he wouldn't hold me responsible for paying the mortgage when I had moved out. He didn't want to do this.

I then came up with a plan. Our business bank manager at RBS was also our personal bank manager so I knew him quite well. I went to see him and asked if the bank would provide me with a loan to buy a flat in the city centre. I told him it was for one of my daughters who was just finishing as a student and wanted to move to Manchester. She was not able to get any credit as she didn't have an income yet so I would buy the flat for her to live in.

Luckily the bank manager agreed so a loan was arranged. Of course I told him that the flat was for me just as soon as I was able. The practical things in life were sometimes difficult. I needed to set up my own bank account. Can you believe that I had never had my own account, it was always a joint account which seems a bit amazing to me now! I needed a copy of the bank statements to open my account. I also needed my passport for identification purposes. I couldn't find it. As usual I just took every day as it came and got on with things with a dogged determination. I applied for a new passport which was easier than I thought. I said I had lost it, which of course I had.

I kept up my flying trips with friends about once a month in order to keep my licence current and myself in practice. At this time of year the weather is not always good enough for VFR flights.

MOVES AND CHANGES

Things seemed to be moving agonisingly slowly. Talkland's accountants came into our business to start the 'due diligence'. This didn't attract too much attention as we had worked fairly closely as two separate companies up to this point. We were always doing joint deals together.

On the personal front I was looking at furniture for my new flat. I had decided to go fairly basic and priced up all the things I needed in flat pack from Ikea. It wasn't a large flat so I didn't need a lot. Only one bedroom, a small bathroom and a kitchen off the living room. The big advantage was that the living room was L Shaped so most of the space in the flat was in the main room. It also had a bay window with a floor to ceiling window. The flat got sun all day so was very cheap to heat.

One of the things I bought was a 'starter pack' of kitchen stuff. It consisted of four of everything, dinner plates, small plates, bowls mugs, cutlery, etc. I confess that I still have most of this stuff now although I have added to it as necessary.

I finally got the keys on 14th March 1994. Apart from odd bedsits as a student, this was the first time I had lived on my own. It was BLISS. I hadn't lived in a flat in my adult years, so it was quite a change from the large houses I had been used to. However I stayed in Venice Court happily for ten years and never felt cramped.

***

I didn't want to disrupt Chris's life more than I had to. I only took my clothes and some books with me. It was agreed between us that I would take the records (vinyl stuff, as it is called now!) and Chris would keep the photographs.

I decided I wanted to make new friends who only knew me as a single person. I would leave all our

Didsbury group of friends for Chris. He needed them, I didn't. If I occasionally met them they would only want to talk about Chris. They still only saw me as Chris's wife.

One couple of friends did stay in touch with both of us. Gary and Mirelle, who lived in West Yorkshire. Gary had worked for us as a contractor for many years so I knew him very well. They also both recognised me as an individual and not half a couple. I had asked Gary to help me with the move as I trusted him and he was very discrete. He hired a van and we went out to Ikea at Warrington with my large shopping list.

**

You can tell a lot about people by their personal language. Some people will refer to their husband or wife as their 'other half' or even their 'better half'. This is amazing. I have always considered myself to be a WHOLE PERSON.

Indeed Germaine Greer wrote a book which was published in 1999 entitled 'The Whole Woman'. It was described by the Guardian as "A Polemic Bomb". Naturally I have it on my bookshelves and probably need to re-read it.

When I was working at the Bridgewater Hall as a

Volunteer Front of House Steward, we often had trouble giving away leaflet hand-outs or gifts at the end of a concert. Couples would always insist they only needed one of anything between them! So our audience number estimates were always inaccurate due to the large number of 'half people' attending.

Once we had a survey to give out about the concert. I tried to give one to a woman who declined saying that her husband had taken one. But you can have one too, I said. We want to know your views as well. She told me that they had the same views and he knew her views so could fill in the form! Is it any wonder that women are treated as door mats if they behave as door mats and delegate all responsibility for life choices to their partners?

Women are often belittled by being referred to as a GIRL. When walking in the Lake District with another woman friend going up Coniston Old Man, we met two men who said, "Hello Girls. Are you going all the way to the top?" In a condescending sort of way. Of course we were. I would often counter this by saying "Hello Boys", which they didn't really like, unsurprisingly.

One of the things I had to learn was to say "I" and not "we". It had become a habit that I needed to change.

Once I had moved into my flat, or PAD as some

of my friends called it, life became easier in some ways. I had my own space so was able to make my own decisions about food and other essentials. I spent the first few weeks assembling furniture in the evenings. A very relaxing occupation. When I needed a break I would go down to the swimming pool to have a swim and relax in the sauna.

Living on your own is the ultimate indulgence. You only have yourself to please. I could decide to go to the cinema in the evening then a friend would phone and after a long chat I could change my mind about going out if I had missed the start of the film. Something that is difficult to do if two people are involved in the decision. I have also found that single people are more sociable with others as they have to make an effort to see friends and not just stay at home with a partner.

From my flat in Venice Court, I had three cinemas within walking distance. Melanie gave me a list of films to see as I had not been to the cinema for years. I was still working full time so sometimes I over did things by going out too much in the evenings. I fell asleep during Oceans 11. When I woke up everyone around me was saying they hadn't anticipated the ending. I had missed the main plot twist. I hope I didn't snore!

I love going to films or plays on my own. If I am not enjoying it I can leave without having to consult anyone else.

One evening I had missed the 8.00pm film showing, so decided to go to the 11.00pm thinking naively that it would be very quiet. It wasn't. Living in the centre of town was a revelation to me. People were starting their evenings when I had previously been going to bed!

***

I now flew fairly regularly with friends or on my own whenever the weather and time around work allowed. I flew with Ruth, her husband Peter, Sue, Dave, Gordon, Mike and Ted.

I flew to Blackpool with Ruth which was always a good scenic trip and back via Sleap. In July I flew to Exeter with Mike and did an hour's instrument flying. This was very easy to do as there is an airway which runs straight down from Liverpool overhead Cardiff and directly on to Exeter. It was good instrument practice for me. The whole flight time was 2 hours 10 minutes.

Exeter Airport is 4 miles east of the city of Exeter. It was officially opened on 31st May 1937 and was originally a 'tented airport' as large tents were used until the terminal buildings were completed. During WW2 it was an important Fighter Command Airfield and active in the Battle of Britain.

Squadrons 203, 87 and 601 were based at Exeter. Three squadrons of the Polish Airforce also used the airfield as a base and are commemorated on brass plaques in the airport observation lounge for their efforts to protect the city of Exeter.

In spite of attempts to camouflage the airport including painting the runways, it was extensively bombed by the Luftwaffe who destroyed the technical and administrative buildings.

After the war the airport handled commercial flights as a busy regional hub. Flybe and Ryanair operated from the airport with flights reaching a peak in 2018/19 of over 1 million passengers. However numbers declined and in March 2020 Flybe went into administration due to curbs on flights during the Coronavirus Pandemic.

In August I flew to Coventry with Dave. I also did some instrument flying with Ed Pape using the ILS at Manchester on runway 06.

In October I flew with Ruth to Nottingham in strong crosswinds. After that there is nothing in my log book until February 95 when I did a check out in G-BOIL another Cessna 172.

There were a number of reasons for this short flying break.

Tango Papa was having a new engine fitted during

this period which Ted supervised. I remember that we bought it from Yorkshire Light Aircraft who were based at Leeds Bradford Airport.

Chris and I had managed to sell the business by this time, so I took a month's holiday to India in November 94.

Although Talkland had bought our business they kept both of us employed under contract for a twelve month period and did not pay the whole amount of monies due until the end of this period. This is a normal procedure which makes sure that nothing nasty comes out of the woodwork of which the buyer is unaware.

Most things in life are easier to get into than to get out of. Certainly setting up a business is easier than selling it, particularly if like us you want to get a good deal for your staff.

NOTE: other things which are easier to get into than out of are

1.   *marriage*

2.   *owning a boat!!*

See my book *(details at end of this book)*

LIGHT THE BLUE TOUCH PAPER – a woman's adventures at sea. *For more about buying, living on and subsequently selling a boat.*

As I was starting to meet new people I now decided to change my name back to Sharp. My married name of Smith had caused some problems, e.g, there were two Smiths in my group at college. The qualification we studied for was a National Diploma in Hotel Keeping and Catering, so when we had finished the exams the papers were sent to a national centre for marking. Before the papers were returned a list was sent to the college showing our marks and Pass/Fail status.

There was a mistake on the list showing that my friend Jenny Smith had passed and I had failed. However when the papers were returned to the college the mistake was revealed. Although it had been a problem for me to tell people I had failed, it was more of a problem for Jenny who had already told friends and family that she had passed and then had to reveal that she had failed.

When Chris and I married we discussed the option of changing his surname so that I would take his name and any children we had would take our surname. However Chris's mother, Kay, heard about this and was cross. She said that Smith was good enough for her and for Chris's father and was therefore good enough for Chris. That was the end of that idea!

In some ways the name change was easy. When I got bills for utilities, etc. through the post I merely contacted the sender and said that I had changed my surname. Most changed the bill name with no questions asked, some assuming I had got married!

The only two organisations I had a problem with were my bank and the CAA who issued my Pilot's Licence. Both of these wanted to see a divorce certificate before changing my surname.

Amazingly the bank said I would need to change my name by Deed Poll. I pointed out that this would not be necessary as I have a birth certificate in the name of Sharp and did not change my name by Deed Poll when I got married. Being a volunteer adviser at Citizens Advice Bureau meant that I was aware of when it was necessary to change a name by Deed Poll.

CHAPTER 15

SINGLE LIFE

Now that I was a single person living on my own I could decide where to go on holiday. As previously mentioned, I had always wanted to go to India but couldn't find anyone who wanted to come with me. India was not a country I wanted to wander around on my own.

It was Chris who told me about small group travel companies like Exodus and Explore. I got the Exodus brochure and was completely hooked. This was just what I wanted. I decided I could spend the rest of my life working my way through the brochure. It was very cheap, eco and basic.

At the time Exodus was a rather small organisation. The company was started in 1974 when two guys John Gillies and David Burlinson took an overland truck to the Hindu Kush. This was the hippie era when people wanted more exploration in small groups for travelling together. Exodus has since expanded with different brochures for walking, cycling and families as well as the overland trucks and has been taken over by larger travel companies.

I carefully chose my first trip which was an India/Nepal overland trip from Bombay (now Mumbai) to Kathmandu and all places in between over the course of a month. The trips were cheap. Exodus used basic local hotels and accommodation. There were two drivers/guides who organised us and managed the kitties for lunches en route which were mostly prepared on the truck. They also drove the large Mercedes truck which was specially kitted out for Exodus travels.

Food in the evenings was very cheap as most of the hotels only served vegetarian food and no alcohol. We were given strict instructions about what to eat and not eat with the result that very few of us suffered from any stomach upsets.

My daughter Melanie came on the trip with me. She was a student in Hull at the time and had come over to Manchester to stay with me in my new city centre pad. I had already booked my trip and she looked with interest through the brochure. As she was finishing her course in the summer and hadn't got a permanent job it was a good time for her to come. I said I would pay for her but was initially a bit concerned as to how she would cope. I insisted she read the itinerary giving the details of the early starts and long days in an open truck over unmade roads. I booked her on the trip and we shared a room. We didn't tell anyone that we were mother and daughter. We were just Philippa and Melanie. Nobody found out for a long time!

This brings to mind a situation when we were out together in a pub in Manchester with a number of Melanie's friends. It must have been dark in the pub as one of the chaps was chatting me up. When I went to visit the loo, he turned to Melanie and said, "so how do you know Philippa?"

When Melanie explained that I was her mother, he looked horrified and fled. He was nowhere to be seen when I returned from the loo!

The trip to India was wonderful. Every day we saw amazing places. The group of us totalled 19 and got on very well keeping in touch for many years afterwards.

***

When I returned to the office, Chris was a bit grumpy as Talkland had put in a manager. Chris said he was asked to give up his office keys but wasn't happy to do this. I said I would be very happy to give up my keys. It would mean that I was no longer on the police call out list for overnight break-ins. These happened frequently and were a nuisance as you could be relaxing at home with a glass of wine or asleep in the early hours and not want to drive to the office, especially as the police would be there when you arrived.

I had enjoyed the India trip so much that I wanted to return over the winter to do the Southern India trip which went from Madras around the south of the country and ended up in Bombay thus completing the All India trip. Neil and Gabrielle who were the drivers/leaders on my first trip were doing the whole season in India. Gabrielle encouraged me to come on the January trip, as Neil's girlfriend, Jackie would be joining him and she would be pleased to have someone she knew to share a room with.

I wasn't sure whether I would be able to take another month away from work and was also worried about my father who had had a minor stroke in January. Chris encouraged me to go. The business now had a new manager in charge so we didn't have much to do. He said he would keep an eye on my parents, so I went off on my travels again.

***

After completing my check out in B-OIL in February I was 'current' again so when Tango Papa was back with the new engine fitted I flew with Mike over to Liverpool and back in order to check it out.

In March 95 I needed to renew my IMC rating so I flew with Ed Pape over to Blackpool doing 1 hour 15 minutes of instrument flying including NDB (Non Directional Beacon) holds on the approach to Warton. Then another 1 hour 10 minutes on instruments in the Blackpool area followed by a flight back from Blackpool to Barton. It was a busy day but my logbook was stamped by Ed with my IMC renewal as satisfactory.

In June I flew with Keiran and several times with Ruth. We often flew together deciding on a destination then one of us would fly there and the other would fly back. We would always meet up in the clubhouse for coffee and then if the weather wasn't good we would just chat.

On 3rd June I flew to Leicester and Ruth flew back. It is a small airfield 4 nm ESE of Leicester. The airfield is operated by Leicestershire Aero Club which was formed in 1909. It offers flying training and is home to many private light aircraft.

CHAPTER 16

GLIDING

On 27th July 95 I flew with Mike to Sutton Bank which is basically a flat hilltop near York.

We went there to watch the National Gliding Championships which were taking place. It was amazing to fly in and see the whole of the hilltop covered in gliders. Aircraft were not allowed to fly in that day. However Mike was given permission as he was famous in the gliding community having won the Championship on more than one occasion. Sutton Bank is not a recognised airstrip so does not feature in the Aerodromes section of Pooleys Flight Guide, however it does appear as a Glider Launching Site.

I have only been gliding once. It was at Long Myndd which is a hilltop in Shropshire near Church Stretton. It is a heath and moorland plateau which is part of the Shropshire hills and is designated as an Area of Outstanding Natural Beauty. The hilltop is 7 miles long and 3 miles wide.

The Long Myndd has been home to the Midland Gliding Club since 1934. The club owns 340 acres of land on the south side and operates gliding throughout the year. It runs residential training courses and offers trial flights to members of the public.

The gliding club is one of the few remaining clubs in Europe which still launches gliders by bungee, a stretchable cord mad of rubber bands.

Launch method – The tail of the glider is tied down or held back; the bungee cord is attached at its mid-point to a hook on the nose of the glider; then a group of people take each end of the cord and when the signal is given they walk, then run with the bungee as hard as they can in opposite directions; when the tension becomes high the tail tie down is released and the glider shoots ahead as though it had been launched by a sling shot. Other and more common glider launch methods are by winch or towing behind a plane.

I went there on a trip with Ruth, and her husband Peter who worked for Barclays Bank. This was an away day event organised by the bank for people to experience gliding.

I don't remember if we were launched by bungee or by towing behind a plane, but I seem to remember it was the winch. A ground-based winch is mounted on a heavy vehicle. A steel wire or synthetic cable of about 1000 – 2500 meters is attached to the front of a glider. As it is wound in the glider rises into the air. The hook is then released when the wire is at an angle of 35 degrees.

It was certainly a very exhilarating experience. I was taken up in a two-seater glider with an experienced glider pilot sitting behind me. While chatting to my pilot companion I mentioned that I had a PPL, so he just said, "ok, you have control".

So I was able to fly the craft. It was very different to Tango Papa. There was one control stick between your legs which could be moved in all directions. Rather like helicopters. The main thing I remember is the complete silence. Very peaceful, except when you had to come in to land – no 'going around' without an engine.

***

VISUAL AIDS TO FLYING

There are many navigational aids around the countryside which people who have not been flying in light aircraft may not be aware of, as a keen hillwalker I often notice these landmarks.

POLE HILL – near Todmorden has a VOR which is visible from a footpath which passes almost alongside the beacon. It is a circular metal structure with spokes going out in a circle from the centre, looking rather like a large metal birthday cake.

VOR stands for VHF (Very high frequency), Omni directional, Radio range.

On one of my walks which I was leading for my Wednesday Ramblers group we stopped for our sandwiches just by this VOR. It was only when I was explaining to some in the group what this structure was, that another walker, Howard realised that I had been a pilot. He is still currently flying so we often have chats about our flying experiences and many of the instructors and other pilots at Barton who are known to both of us.

TELEVISION MASTS

EMLEY MOOR *is a very noticeable mast near Huddersfield. It is quite 'fat' and stands out on the hillside near the Village of Emley. The concrete tower that you see there today is the third structure to be on this site. It is 1084 feet high and is a Grade II listed building. It is the tallest freestanding structure in the UK, 66 feet taller than the Shard in London, which is the next tallest.*

The original lattice structure of 443 feet was installed in 1956 and broadcast television programmes for Granada Television. In 1964 it was replaced by a guyed mast 1265 feet high. This mast had constant problems with ice forming on the metal guys in winter. Warning notices were posted nearby as large pieces of ice would fall from the guys. Warning lights were also used to flash when falling ice was possible.

On 19th March 1969 a combination of strong winds with ice on the tower and supporting wire guys caused the mast to collapse. Luckily no-one was injured although a falling cable cut through a nearby church. Over 2.5 million people were without TV reception for a time while a temporary mast was brought into place. Some VHF transmissions continued from Holme Moss.

WINTER HILL.

Located on Rivington Moor in North West England, Winter Hill is 1496 feet at its highest point and part of the West Pennine Moors. It is the perfect location for a transmitter mast which is visible for miles around. It is 11 nm north of Barton and just above the town of Bolton.

The mast is a dominant feature of the landscape when driving north from Manchester up the M61 but is also useful to pilots for orientation purposes. I remember that on one of my IMC lessons when I was instructed to remove my foggles, I was level with the mast and approaching it fast! I had to take avoiding action fairly quickly. I think the instructor found this amusing.

The area is well known for some excellent walks

with good views often right out to the coast at Blackpool, where the tower is visible.

The original mast on Winter Hill was a 450 foot tower which came into service on 5ᵗʰ May 1956. The mast transmitted the TV services for Granada TV and ABC weekend TV. From 1966 a new mast came into service which was 1015 feet tall. This was constructed next to the original mast and is used for the new digital service.

Winter Hill is the principal transmitter for the Granada region and in 2009 became the first in the UK to broadcast digital TV in High Definition. FM and DAB radio channels are also broadcast from the transmitter.

WINTER HILL PLANE CRASH DISASTER

On 27ᵗʰ February 1958 a plane travelling from the Isle of Man to Manchester in severe weather crashed into the hill a few hundred yards away from the mast. 35 people were killed, 7 survived but were injured. The weather was so bad that engineers working at the mast were unaware of the crash due to the noise of the storm. The snow was so deep that a snow cat vehicle had to be diverted to cut a path through the snow for emergency vehicles to help the rescue attempts.

Subsequent flying trips during the rest of 1995 included a trip to Shobdon airfield which is 9 nm west of Leominster. It is operated by Herefordshire Aero Club.

The airfield started life as a British Army camp and received casualties from the evacuation of Dunkirk which were brought in via Southampton. It was further developed in 1943 by the United States Army and a runway was added.

The no. 1 RAF glider training school moved to Shobdon from RAF Thame and glider pilots were trained in preparation for the landings at Normandy and Arnhem.

I also flew to Rush Green, near Hitchin and back via Gloucester with Mike. Gloucestershire Airport is 3.5 nm west of Cheltenham. It was formerly known as Staverton. It is now home to several private flying clubs – Bristol Aero Club and Cotswold Aero Club as well as Staverton Flying School and JK Helicopter Training.

Flights in 1996 included Walney Island and Caernarfon, but on 15th June 96 which was a famous date, I made a memorable trip to Carlisle.

CHAPTER 17

MANCHESTER BOMB

It was a beautiful sunny day on Saturday 15th June 1996. The city centre of Manchester was full of shoppers as it was the day before Father's Day - Sunday 16th June.

I had planned a flight to Carlisle with Mike and Vicky. We took off from Barton at 11.40. I flew there. We had glorious views up over Cumbria and the Lake District hills. Flying time was 1.05. When we arrived we went for tea at the airport café. I remember sitting outside at one of the tables in the sun when I received a phone call from one of my daughters. She asked me where I was, then told me that a bomb had gone off in Manchester City Centre.

During this era the IRA (Irish Republican Army) were conducting a terror campaign in England. Large cities were often targets. As both my daughters lived in London we would always call each other if there were bombs in the areas where we lived. Once a bomb went off in a pub where Sam had gone regularly with work colleagues on a Friday lunchtime, however on this occasion they had been in a meeting so were not able to go to the pub.

I told Sam that I was in Carlisle so was safe. The extent of the damage and number of casualties were unknown at this stage.

This was in the days before I had a smart phone so we didn't linger and stare at screens for news, instead we set off south with Mike flying back this time over the Lake District with wonderful views of Lake Windermere and the coast at Morecambe Bay.

Vicky was concerned about her mother who lived in a residential home in south Manchester. Vicky had not wanted to tell her mother that she was going for a flight in a small aircraft in case she worried, so unfortunately she had said she was going shopping in town!

The IRA had detonated a 1500 kg lorry bomb on Corporation Street in the heart of the shopping district in Manchester City Centre. It was the biggest bomb detonated in the UK since the Second World War.

There had been a phone call warning about the bomb 90 minutes before the explosion, so although the Bomb Squad was not able to diffuse the bomb there were over 75,000 people evacuated from the area. Apart from the sunny day England was hosting the Euro 96 Football championships so people were crowding into bars and pubs to watch the matches.

The bombing was condemned by the British and Irish governments and US President Bill Clinton. It was 6 days after the bombing that the IRA claimed responsibility but said they regretted any civilian casualties. Although 200 people were injured there were no fatalities.

Extensive damage to the city's infrastructure and economy was estimated by insurers to be £700 million. Several buildings had to be demolished due to irreparable damage.

*** *

When we had landed, parked up and tied down Tango Papa we departed in separate directions. Mike went home, Vicky went to see her mother and I went back into town to see what the situation was. Vicky and I both lived in the city centre.

I couldn't get to the carpark at my flat in Granby Village as it was cordoned off by a police barricade. I needed to drive out of town until I could find somewhere to park then head in again on foot. The Euro 96 match scheduled to be played in Manchester was between Russia and Germany so many foreign football fans were around. As the city centre had been evacuated and cordoned off, lots of people were filling the pubs outside the cordon. People were sitting on the pavements in the sun. It was in sharp contrast to the scene in the centre.

I went boldly up to a policewoman at the barricade and asked if I could go in to my flat. She said I could but it was at my own risk. There were still fears that there may have been other bombs. Venice Court was deserted and eerily quiet. I didn't linger for long. I checked that my flat was ok, then collected some clothes and the keys to a cottage I owned in Kirkby Lonsdale. Luckily it was empty that weekend, as I sometimes managed to let it for holidays.

I then returned to my car and drove north to Kirkby Lonsdale where I stayed for the weekend, keeping an eye on the news. When the city centre had been checked the barricaded area was reduced to the damaged site around Cross Street, Market Street and Deansgate, so there was access to my flat and underground car park. I was then able to return home.

It was extremely sad to see the destruction. I went for a walk around the centre and saw the damage around Market Street and Corporation Street where the lorry bomb had been parked. There is a red post box across the road from the site of the bomb. It was unscathed. It is still there today and has a plaque on it commemorating the bomb damage and the survival of the post box.

Windows of many buildings as far as Deansgate had been shattered. The Royal Exchange Theatre had been extensively damaged. It was one of my favourite buildings in Manchester centre.

The first exchange was built on this site in 1809. It traded in cotton and other textiles. After a visit in 1851 by Queen Victoria it was granted the title of the Royal Exchange. At its peak there was a membership of 11,000 cotton merchants who met on Tuesdays and Fridays to trade.

Due to expansion of the cotton trade larger premises were needed so a new building was built on the site between 1867 and 1874. In 1914 modifications were done to the building and it was opened in 1921. The original trading floor known as the Grand Hall was twice the size of today's space, but was damaged in the Manchester Blitz in 1940.

Trading continued until 1968 when the last figures at the closure were left on the board on the wall. These historical figures were damaged in the 1996 bomb.

In 1973 a theatre company took up residence in the building and in 1976 the Royal Exchange Theatre Company opened its doors to the public.

After the bomb damage in 1996 the building was

closed until 1998 while it was repaired. There are many shops and businesses around and even under the building, so all services needed repairing and safety checks on gas and water pipes.

CHAPTER 18

MORE FLYING TRIPS

Many other flights were fairly uneventful. I only remembered the odd happenings, e.g. I flew with Ted to Liverpool in May. I had not remembered this trip until I met Ted recently to borrow some charts and other stuff from him. He reminded me of the time we flew into Liverpool and had 'conversations' with an air traffic controller whose first language was not English.

He would say something over the radio and we both stared at each other in confusion. "What did he say?" Neither of us had a clue. I think he was Russian, but he certainly had a very strong accent which made it hard to understand what he had said. Luckily we must have had the right information as we landed successfully and also departed back to Barton afterwards.

In July I flew with Ruth to Tatenhill and Welshpool. I have noted in my logbook that it was very hot. Ruth reminded me recently that the brakes were stuck on due to the heat when we tried to taxi back to the runway. I was the one who was flying back from Welshpool to Barton. We went to have a cup of tea and allow the wheels to cool a little, which seemed to sort the problem.

Tatenhill Airfield is 6 miles west of Burton on Trent. It is part of the Needwood Survey, a 3000 hectare estate owned by the Duchy of Lancaster. The airfield was constructed in 1941 using the standard RAF construction of three runways in a triangle.

In 1987 it was taken over by Tatenhill Aviation. The airfield was licenced in the 1990s and a flying school was set up. The Midland Air Ambulance is currently based there.

Welshpool Aerodrome is situated in the River Severn Valley 2 miles south of Welshpool town. There is high ground on each side of the valley. Pilots are advised not to descend below safety height until final approach when the runway has been positively identified. The runway was changed in 1990 from a grass strip to the present day tarmac runway of 1020m long.

There are three flying clubs offering instruction on fixed wing, helicopters and microlight aircraft. It is also the Mid Wales base for the Wales Air Ambulance.

In August I took a trip up to Cumbernauld. I cannot remember who with, but it must have been another fellow pilot, as I have only noted my return trip from Cumbernauld which took 2.05 hours.

The purpose of the trip was for me to get some photographs of a holiday property that Chris and I were letting on the shores of Loch Tay. It was a wonderful clear day and the photos came out very well.

Cumbernauld Airport is 16 nm NE of Glasgow. It is a small airport and is mainly used for training flights of fixed wing and rotary wing aircraft but also has a small charter flight operation. The airport is beneath the Scottish Controlled airspace so aircraft must stay below 2500 ft. You can join overhead at 2000 ft and circuit height is 1000 ft.

In October I flew with Mike and Simon to Blackbushe. I was flying the return leg and did 50 minutes instrument flying on a total flight of 1.15 hours. As a pilot you were constantly learning and renewing any ratings you have achieved. I was well aware that my IMC renewal was coming up.

Blackbushe Airport is 2 nm W of Camberley. Built during the Second World War, Blackbushe is just north of the A30 road from Camberley to Hook. For a time the airfield straddled the road and traffic often had to wait while aircraft were towed across, as the south side was used for maintenance in disused wartime hangars. Today the airfield is only active on the north side of the A30. The airport is open to the public and the area is a popular one with walkers due to the wildlife in Yateley common and the Castle Bottom National Nature Reserves.

***

On 8th November 97 I did a Full Panel revision with Martin Rushbrooke, with SRA (Surveillance Radar Approach).

On 3rd March 97 I did a day's flying with Martin including my IMC Rating Renewal Flight Test.

Throughout 1997 I continued flying with friends and fellow pilots to various airfields both new and familiar favourites. As Tango Papa was a four-seater plane we could take a friend along with two of us flying as well. I mostly flew with Ruth and we would sometimes take another person in the back. Taking four people was not a good idea. You had to do a weight and balance check, as the plane sloped downwards at the tail. If you had two heavy people in the back it could cause vibration and wobbling during take-off.

WALNEY ISLAND

I had often flown to Walney Island. The airfield there is 1.5 nm NW of Barrow in Furness. It is operated by BAE Systems and has the typical triangle shape with three runways. This design originally developed by the RAF gave the maximum possibility of landing without cross wind. The airfield was opened in 1935 for military purposes during WW2. It was owned by the council after the war before being purchased by Vickers in 1968.

Although Walney is an island, it is now joined to Barrow Island by the Jubilee Bridge. This bridge was constructed when the planned development of Vickerstown was built to house workers for Vickers Shipbuilding and Engineering Works. The bridge was opened in 1908, it is a bascule bridge which has a counterweight to allow it to move in order to accommodate marine traffic.

The island also has two nature reserves, one at either end, and the sandy beaches make it a popular leisure destination. It is also home to the Walney Bird Observatory.

It is narrow, low lying and windy. Visually very easy to find on a flight as it sticks out at the western end of Morecambe Bay, but due to the amount of water you have to fly over a plane needs to be at a height of 3,000 feet in order to observe the 'land clear' rule. This covers the possibility of an engine failure when over water so that your plane is high enough to glide to an area where you could safely land.

CHAPTER 19

GORDON

Gordon was another student pilot I met when I started training with MSF at Manchester Airport. We kept in touch while studying and after we qualified.

When I was flying at Barton, Gordon would often come over and fly on trips with me. He lived in Huddersfield and flew out of Crosland Moor.

Crosland Moor is a small privately owned airfield. It is 1.5nm SW of Huddersfield, up on a hill so often windy. The runway is part asphalt and part grass. There is a slope of 2.6% downwards on runway 07. It is surrounded by quarries at the threshold of runway 25 so pilots are advised to land well beyond the threshold.

It is an unlicensed aerodrome operated by Huddersfield Aviation Ltd. Due to the terrain and runway type, it is generally pretty scary going in there. Real seat of the pants stuff.

I have only noted flying into Crosland Moor once which was in June 1998. Gordon was with me, which was obviously good to have a local pilot for advice. Gordon was a good engineer and liked to do the maintenance on his own planes. He was able to do this as he owned a Tipsy Nipper, which is a small single seater microlight so covered by different regulations from Tango Papa which is a four-seater class A aircraft.

Sadly Gordon was killed in an accident in his plane on 16th July 2000. His wife phoned me to let me know but was so emotional and upset about it that she was unable to tell me what happened. I had to ask Mike who also knew Gordon if he could find out the circumstances for me.

Gordon had an engine failure when coming back to Crosland Moor. He managed to get the plane down into a field, but a Tipsy Nipper has a small-wheeled tricycle type undercarriage which is not very stable so on the rough uneven field it flipped over. Having a perspex domed hood on top this caused damage to Gordon's head.

While researching for this book I googled the details and found the CAA report of the accident. The CAA give very thorough reports on all reported accidents which examine everything from the plane, the weather and the pilot. I often think about Gordon and how he must have felt when he got the plane down into the field and probably felt relief and satisfaction before it turned over and killed him.

CHAPTER 20

CONCORDE

The week after Gordon's accident there was another aviation accident with many more deaths. On 25th July 2000 an Air France Concorde crashed two minutes after take-off in Paris. It burst into flames and crashed on a hotel in Gonesse killing all 109 passengers and crew on board as well as 6 people in the hotel on the ground.

Concorde was a very iconic aeroplane and was operated by both Air France and British Airways. It only held 100 passengers and was narrow inside as it was designed to fly at very high speeds making the transatlantic flight to New York at supersonic speeds. It was considered to be a very safe plane and this was the only crash in its 27 years of service.

An investigation into the crash blamed a metal strip on the runway which fell from the Continental Airlines DC10 which had taken off 5 minutes before Concorde. This damaged Concorde's tyre which sent debris upwards to the fuel tanks and ruptured them causing fuel to pour downwards igniting the fire.

The findings of the investigation were controversial as other factors appeared to have contributed to the accident including the fact of the plane being overloaded and previous incidents with tyres and wheels being damaged. Continental Airlines was held criminally responsible and a court case found the company guilty. There was subsequently an appeal which overturned the verdict as witnesses claimed the plane was on fire before it reached the strip on the runway. There have been many interesting documentaries about this crash.

All Concordes were grounded for investigation after this and modifications were made, but regular flights did not resume on the same scale as before. The last Concordes flew in 2003 and can now only be seen in museums.

***

CONCORDE AT MANCHESTER AIRPORT

A Concorde is now resident at the Runway Visitor Park at Manchester Airport. This is G-BOAC which was the second Concorde to be delivered to British Airways in 1976. Concorde was the world's first supersonic airliner. Although considered to be the flagship of the fleet it was in commercial service for 27 years.

One of my grandsons, Will is very keen on all things 'transport', so we have done many excursions to

York Railway Museum, the Bury to Ramsbottom steam railway, London Transport Museum, HMS Belfast and the Manchester Transport Museum.

When he visited me in Manchester we would often go on the Metro. As the tram lines increased, we needed to travel on every line and cover the whole of the developing network. So it was natural that when he came to stay with me in October 2018 we took a trip to the Visitor Park at Manchester Airport. I had booked two tours for us both on Concorde and Nimrod.

The Concorde is now housed in its own hangar so there is plenty of space for viewing it both inside and outside. The tour took us around and underneath Alpha Charlie. It was a lengthy tour and for transport enthusiasts like Will and I, much of it was information we already knew, but it was fascinating to go inside the plane.

It is very small and narrow in the passenger cabin as there are only two seats either side of the isle. Concorde had capacity for 100 passengers. However the time spent in the cabin during flights is shorter than most transatlantic flights as it only took three hours to travel from London Heathrow to New York JFK.

Displays for the passengers show the MACH number, so if 2.00 was displayed the aircraft was flying at twice the speed of sound. Other displays showed height, DTG (distance to go) and speed.

Everyone was allowed to go into the cockpit and sit in the left-hand pilot's seat. We were shown the switch which would lower the visor (covering the windscreen for protection) then two settings to lower the nose for giving the pilots vision for taxiing when on the ground.

We were both given Boarding Certificates to commemorate our visit and tour of Concorde. We also toured the RAF Nimrod which is retired from active service in the Falklands, Afghanistan and Iraq. These were active war zones from the 1970s to 2010.

Nimrod was a specialist Search and Rescue aircraft. This tour was very interesting as we knew less about the plane. Not many people take this tour so there was a lot more space to move around and ask questions.

Other aircraft at the Visitors Park include a fully restored BEA Trident G-AWZK. This plane has been at the park since 2003 and has 23,000 flying hours on the clock. It was the first aircraft to make a fully automated approach and landing.

***

Only 20 Concordes were built. Of these, one crashed, one was scrapped and 17 are preserved in museums and aviation parks and can be visited. Of these there are 7 in the UK, 6 in France, 1 in Germany and 3 in the US.

N.B. There is one in Barbados but it can no longer be visited.

CHAPTER 21

LAST FLIGHT

By 1998 I realised that my nine years of flying were drawing to a close. There were a number of reasons for this. Ruth had stopped flying and sold her share in Tango Papa, which was a blow for me as I had enjoyed flying with her.

The medical situation grew increasingly stricter with age. When I was flying I had a Class 3 Medical Certificate. (There does not appear to be a Class 3 Certificate anymore, only Class 1 and 2.)

These certificates were valid for different lengths of time depending on the pilot's age.

1. Under 40 – 60 months

2. 40 to 49 – 24 months

3. 50 to 69 – 12 months

4. 70 and over – 6 months

The Medical Certificate could only be issued by an AME (aeromedical examiner) not just a GP so was obviously expensive. It was a very thorough examination and included things like a 'strength test' and an ECG (electrocardiogram).

My certificate was stamped stating that it was VALID ONLY WHILE WEARING CORRECTING SPECTACLES WITH A SECOND PAIR AVAILABLE.

This obviously made sense. You cannot simply stop flying if you lose or break your specs. You need them to make a landing. I always kept a spare pair in my flight bag.

At Barton there were a number of Portakabins which were used as classrooms, interview rooms and for examinations. There was an AME who visited and would carry out medicals in one of these Portakabins.

I did not like this situation at all. There were no locks on doors and some clothing needed to be removed during medical examinations. As already stated there were very few women pilots, so the men probably were not concerned about the lack of privacy. Although a notice 'Medical examination in progress' was put on the door, many people would just ignore it and barge in. If a urine sample was required you would have to take your sample pot over to the loos in the clubhouse.

Luckily Ted told me about Dr Kerns, an AME who was based in Worsley. This was a much better situation. It was professional and private.

So having medicals was an expensive procedure and would become more so if I continued to fly after 70. However I developed high blood pressure in my 60s (a family history problem, nothing to do with life style) so I probably would not have passed the medicals anyway!

My last medical was issued on 29.10.98.

***

Another reason to stop flying was that I had been to a lot of places over the years.

Since 1989 I had visited 35 different aerodromes apart from my home bases of Manchester Airport and Barton.

I enjoyed having a purpose to my flights and a sense of achievement. Some pilots, like Ted can just enjoy going up for a spin and putting the plane through a series of exercises and manoeuvres. I didn't. So I was reaching the limits of places to fly to.

I didn't want to fly over water in a single engine, so going to the Continent, Isle of Man or Ireland was not something I would feel safe doing. Morecambe Bay was enough for me. When I look at the places I have been in the UK from Bournemouth and Exeter on the south coast to Swansea and Caernarfon in the West of Wales, Aberdeen and

Gigha in Scotland, I think I was more adventurous than many PPLs at Barton.

As with everything, you need to know when to stop.

However I was still only 51. I had more adventures left in me and was feeling the need for a new one. During January 1998 I had been on holiday in the Grenadines for my birthday and noticed the small sail boats bobbing around in the harbour at Union Island. They seemed small and I wondered what it would be like to live on one. Could this be a new adventure for me?

I figured that if I could fly a plane then I could sail a boat. So by the summer of 1998 I had completed a Competent Crew certificate and spent a month in Bequia doing 'boat research' mainly in bars.

The last flight in my logbook was on 19.9.98 when I flew with Judy from Barton up to Kirkby Lonsdale and back.

CHAPTER 22

SUMMARY AND CONCLUSIONS

WOMEN'S LIB, FEMINISM, ETC.

Many changes were happening in the 60s and 70s to the lives of young people in England. It was called the Swinging Sixties. Notable figures like Michael Caine, David Bailey, Marianne Faithful, The Beatles, The Rolling Stones, Mary Quant and Twiggy set the scene for previously underprivileged people from a working class background to become successful.

This was also reflected in the surge of Women's Liberation issues highlighted by writers like Germaine Greer. I recently read a book by Helen Lewis 'Difficult Women' in which she calls this surge the Second Wave. I had never heard this expression. Presumably the First Wave was the Suffragettes movement who campaigned to get the vote for women. However Equality for Women has never gone away, like the waves at sea which are sometimes small but never cease unless it is flat calm. I don't think this will be achieved in my lifetime so it is an endless fight, not just a wave.

When leaving college I applied for a management training scheme at ICI. I was told at the interview that women would start at 80% of the male salary.

If we were good we could build up to 100%. If you are not sure about equality issues it may help to substitute 'black people' in the place of 'women'. E.g. How would that look for black people?

After my retirement and sailing adventures I became a volunteer at Citizens Advice, Women's Domestic Abuse Helpline and a Magistrate. Naturally I was quite involved with women's issues in these roles.

At my first interview at the Magistrates Court I was asked whether I believed in Women's Liberation – how could any woman not be? Then I was asked if I believed in women's only short lists. I don't. When I became a Magistrate I was not allowed to sit in the Domestic Violence Courts on a Wednesday. I think this was because I was working on the WDAH helpline. They thought I might not be impartial to violence from both sexes. However so many of our cases in all the courts involved DV issues, from criminal damage and assault to harassment and stalking.

Germaine Greer in her book 'The Whole Woman' quotes Margaret Atwood who asked a group of men why they found women threatening. 'We're afraid that women will laugh at us', they said. And she asked a group of women why they felt threatened by men. 'We're afraid of being killed', they said.

In the UK two women a week are killed by partners/ex partners. I believe this is just the tip of the iceberg. These are only the cases which come to court. Many women's deaths are listed as suicide or accidental death. There are also 'honour killings' which are only another name for murder.

While I was working at the helpline a march was organised during a week's campaign highlighting Violence Against Women. The banners read 'Together We Can Stop Violence Against Women'. I didn't go on the march. This statement is wrong. The only people who can stop violence against women are men. Maybe it is time somebody talked to men about this?

***

When I started writing this book I intended it to be purely about my flying experiences, but the more I looked at my life during these nine years I realised how much it had changed.

At the beginning in 1989 I was married, living at home with two children and running a business with Chris, my husband. By the end in 1998, I was divorced, living on my own, my daughters had left home and Chris and I had sold the mobile communications business. I felt ready for a change with some fun and indulgence. Although for me it had to be learning new things as well, something I thrived on.

I told the others in the Tango Papa group that I was intending to buy a boat and go out to the Caribbean for a period of time – I didn't know how long, so felt it would not be wise to keep the share I had in the plane. It was not economical to the upkeep if one member of the group was not flying as we paid per flying hour. Also I would not be able to keep 'current' which would not be safe.

I now wonder if the title of this book was significant apart from the fact that I made a parachute jump. Did it signify that making a jump from the plane into the unknown, was like the leap out of my marriage to make a big change in my life? This change may well have happened anyway and not be anything to do with learning to fly. Who knows, but certainly the flying training took me to new places, I met new people and I achieved things which gave me confidence to make the changes I knew I needed.

Some of the experiences in this book were fun, some of them were scary – VERY! Some of the personal ones were painful and distressing, but that's life. It happens and we deal with it in the best way that we can. Would I have wanted to live 'happily ever after' in my marriage? Maybe, but it didn't work out that way. Sometimes life feels like a roller coaster where you just hang on and enjoy the ride in the best way that you can.

***

When I was 50, I met up with some school friends for lunch in Covent Garden. I hadn't seen them since I was 16. I thought I had changed when I left my marriage but they said:

"No, you were always the same, you had the best legs, the best men and you broke all the rules!"

Great. This showed me that I was still the same person. Being in a controlling marriage had just restricted me. Now I had returned to normal.

They then suggested we did what we had done when out of our boarding school for lunch. I couldn't remember what that was. Apparently we didn't pay the bill but all went to the loo one at a time and climbed out of the window.

***

In the years after our divorce, Chris once said to me, "If I had let you do what you wanted to do, would we still be together?"

That rather says it all! He knew what our situation was, and it resulted in our separation.

People tend to think that if you are divorced then your marriage was a failure. This was not true in my case. We lived together for 30 years, we worked in a business together for 15 years, we have two daughters and four grandsons and we all still speak to each other! Marriage is not forever. People grow and change. We have both done different and exciting things since we separated which we would not have done if we stayed together. Chris climbed Mount Kilimanjaro, made two sailing trips on the Tall Ship Tenacious and remarried. I have spent 26 years living on my own, using my city centre flat as a base for various holidays and adventures from time to time.

***

This book is a prequel. It is the account of eleven years in my life from 1987 to 1998. It brought me to the situation I was in at the beginning of 1998 when I went on holiday to the Grenadines to celebrate my birthday in January.

Checking out Tango Papa at Barton

Checking out Sierra India at Faro

So now you can read on with the first book I wrote during the Lockdown in 2020 called

LIGHT THE BLUE TOUCH PAPER
A WOMAN'S ADVENTURES AT SEA

Published by Big White Shed
£9.99 paperback
£2.99 Amazon Kindle

Contact me at
bluetouchpaperbooks@gmail.com
www.philippasharp.com

ACKNOWLEDGEMENTS

My sincere thanks are due to the following people:

Chris Smith – who was involved with every step of the story and helped with the reading and editing of the book. He spent time searching in the family photo archives to find relevant photos and information, giving feed-back on his memories of events and our history together.

Sam – for her input on parachute jumping.

Melanie – for her contribution to my Hull flight memories.

Members of the Tango Papa flying group:

Mike Bond, Ruth O'Halloran and Ted Heath for sharing their input and memories. Ted also lent me charts, check lists and allowed me to include the account of his engine failure.

Howard – for correction of flying details with his current knowledge of Barton and memories of many people at Barton as well.

Mark – for careful reading, editing and advice.

Anne Holloway of Big White Shed – for her enthusiasm, encouragement and hard work in producing this book.